The Ethical Pragmatism of Albert Camus

American University Studies

Series II
Romance Languages and Literature

Vol. 18

PETER LANG
New York · Berne · Frankfurt am Main

Dean Vasil

The Ethical Pragmatism of Albert Camus
Two Studies in the History of Ideas

PETER LANG
New York · Berne · Frankfurt am Main

Library of Congress Cataloging in Publication Data

Vasil, Dean, 1949-
The Ethical Pragmatism of Albert Camus.

(American University Studies. Series II, Romance Languages and Literature; vol. 18)
Bibliography: p.
1. Camus, Albert, 1913–1960 – Criticism and Interpretation. 2. Ethics in Literature. 3. Pragmatism in Literature. 4. Philosophy in Literature. 5. Ethics. 6. Pragmatism. I. Title. II. Series.
PQ2605.A3734Z84   1985   848'.91409   84-48031
ISBN 0-8204-0166-8
ISSN 0740-9257

CIP-Kurztitelaufnahme der Deutschen Bibliothek

Vasil, Dean:
The Ethical Pragmatism of Albert Camus: Two Studies in the History of Ideas / Dean Vasil. – New York; Berne; Frankfurt am Main: Lang, 1985.
(American University Studies: Ser. 2, Romance Languages and Literature; Vol. 18)
ISBN 0-8204-0166-8

NE: American University Studies / 02

© Peter Lang Publishing, Inc., New York 1985

All rights reserved.
Reprint or reproduction, even partially, in all forms such as microfilm, xerography, microfiche, microcard, offset prohibited.

Printed by Lang Druck Inc., Liebefeld/Berne (Switzerland)

ΧΑΙΡΕ, ΣΟΦΩΝ ΥΠΕΡΒΑΙΝΟΥΣΑ ΓΝΩΣΙΝ·
ΧΑΙΡΕ, ΠΙΣΤΩΝ ΚΑΤΑΥΓΑΖΟΥΣΑ ΦΡΕΝΑΣ.
--From The Akathist Hymn,
in honor and gratitude

For My Mother

ACKNOWLEDGMENTS

I knew of the reputation and had read many of the works of my mentor, Professor Henri Peyre, long before it became my privilege to meet and to study with him. His achievement in literary history and in the history of ideas will far outlast that of what he himself has called "l'analyse méticuleuse, et peut-être myope, d'un texte limité, découpé, trituré, déchiffré (ou obscurci) dans les secrets de son 'écriture'."[1] "For him," as Walter Langlois remarks, "the primary value--and joy-- of literature lies less in an appreciation of its structures and techniques than in the insights it may provide into man and his condition."[2] And this, I may add, explains his openmindedness to all of these insights; so that in a recent interview with him Blanche Brossman spoke for me as for every alumnus of the City University of New York when she said that "vous les aidez à se trouver eux-mêmes selon leur voie à eux et à découvrir leur propre vérité."[3]

I would like to thank two readers, Professors Bettina L. Knapp and Rosette C. Lamont, for their invaluable corrections of style, and for their classic lectures, during my first semester at the Graduate School, on the Greek and Hebraic conceptions of history in their memorable course on the Theater of the Apocalypse. Their moving remarks inspired me to pursue my fervent interest in the history of ideas, and to them I here express the esteem of many for their talent and their persons.

To Mrs. Lenore C. Kessler, Administrative Assistant to Professor Peyre, I owe far more than I can say. I will remember her for her professionalism, her integrity, and her selfless dedication to the Program and its students.

Finally, I am deeply indebted to Father Nicholas Katsoulis of the Greek Orthodox Archdiocese of North and South America, for it is through him that I have come to rediscover both the meaning of my own tradition, and that, in my effort, of the divine words, ΟΤΙ ΧΩΡΙΣ ΕΜΟΥ ΟΥ ΔΥΝΑΣΘΕ ΠΟΙΕΙΝ ΟΥΔΕΝ.

Notes

[1] Blanche Brossman, "Entretien avec Henri Peyre," Nineteenth-Century French Studies, 5, Nos. 1-2, La Littérature devant l'Histoire: Essays in Honor of Henri Peyre (Fall-Winter 1976-1977), 20.

[2] Walter G. Langlois, "Henri Peyre and the Nineteenth Century," Nineteenth-Century French Studies, 5, Nos. 1-2, La Littérature devant l'Histoire: Essays in Honor of Henri Peyre (Fall-Winter 1976-1977), 4.

[3] Brossman, art. cit., 20.

CONTENTS

ACKNOWLEDGMENTS ix

GENERAL NOTE AND ABBREVIATIONS xv

INTRODUCTION 1

CHAPTER I. CAMUS AND THE ENLIGHTENMENT: HIS
           PRAGMATIC RATIONALISM 7

CHAPTER II. CAMUS AND EXISTENTIAL PHILOSOPHY:
            HIS TRAGIC REALISM 35

SELECT BIBLIOGRAPHY 109

GENERAL NOTE AND ABBREVIATIONS

On four occasions in the first part of this essay we have used Anthony Bower's translation of L'Homme Révolté, The Rebel: An Essay on Man in Revolt, Vintage Books, 30 (New York: Random House, 1956), in order to facilitate the integration of some of the lines quoted from that work into the body of our text. We have provided the original, however, in each of the notes to the respective quotations. The few other translations of French in both parts of this essay are our own, as will appear obvious from the context or as we will have indicated in notes providing the original for some of these as well. We may also note that part of the epigraph from Rousseau to the first of the two studies in this essay is quoted in Arthur O. Lovejoy, The Great Chain of Being, A Study of the History of an Idea: The William James Lectures Delivered at Harvard University, 1933 (Cambridge: Harvard Univ. Press, 1964), p. 201. Lovejoy's quotation, however, is a translation from the French into English. We have used the original in Emile ou de l'éducation, ed. François and Pierre Richard, Coll. "Classiques Garnier" (Paris: Garnier Frères, 1964), pp. 68, 65.

Finally, we have employed the following system of abbreviations for those works of Camus that we have cited, all of which are collected in Théâtre, Récits, Nouvelles, Bibliothèque de la Pléiade, 161, ed. Roger Quilliot (Paris: Gallimard, 1962); in Essais, Bibliothèque de la Pléiade, 183, ed. Roger Quilliot and Louis Faucon (Paris: Gallimard, 1965); and as Carnets I: mai 1935-février 1942, Collection Soleil, 100, ed. Roger Quilliot (Paris: Gallimard, 1962), and Carnets II: janvier 1942-mars 1951, Collection Soleil, 156, ed. Roger Quilliot (Paris: Gallimard, 1964):

AI   Actuelles I: Chroniques 1944-1948

AII   Actuelles II: Chroniques 1948-1953

CI   Carnets I

CII   Carnets II

CAL   Caligula

CH	La Chute
DS	Discours de Suède
E	L'Etranger
EE	L'Envers et l'Endroit
ER	L'Exil et le Royaume
ES	L'Etat de siège
ESS	"Essais Critiques" and "Textes complémentaires" in Essais
ETE	L'Eté
HR	L'Homme Révolté
J	Les Justes
LAA	Lettres à un ami allemand
MAL	Le Malentendu
MS	Le Mythe de Sisyphe
N	Noces
P	La Peste
TRN	"Textes complémentaires" in Théâtre, Récits, Nouvelles

In addition, the abbreviation EN is used for one of the works of Jean-Paul Sartre that we have frequently cited with those of Camus: L'Etre et le Néant: Essai d'ontologie phénoménologique, Coll. "Bibliothèque des Idées" (Paris: Gallimard, 1943), 722pp. The numbers that follow the abbreviations for most of the works of Camus refer to the pages of the volumes of Essais and Théâtre, Récits, Nouvelles that contain them. Hence the number in (MS: 114) refers to the page of the volume containing Le Mythe de Sisyphe, namely the Essais, while that in (CAL: 16) refers to the page of the volume containing Caligula, namely Théâtre, Récits, Nouvelles (see the first section of our bibliography, infra). The obvious exception to this rule is that of the Carnets, for the numbers that follow their abbreviations refer to the pages of the Carnets themselves, as in (CI: 101), or (CII: 28).

INTRODUCTION

"I claim," writes Bernard-Henri Lévy in <u>Barbarism with a Human Face</u>, "that the antibarbarian intellectual, finally, will be a <u>moraliste</u>, and when I say <u>moraliste</u> I mean it in the classic sense, like Kant, Camus, or Merleau-Ponty."[1] I do <u>not</u> claim as much, for I am as "fully aware" as Lévy of what he himself calls "the secrets and the trickeries of the categorical imperative."[2] But if "the virtues of an atheist spiritualism"[3] were not foreign to me (for I do not consider that "God has been dead since Nietzsche,"[4] nor that He was even dead before him), then I, like Lévy, would "prefer that lie"--the lie, that is, of a moral imperative without God--"to the lie of historicist superstition"[5]--or the lie of "becoming" God in His place. The first is illogical, but the second is irrational, "la prédication de la surhumanité," as Camus says, "aboutissant à la fabrication méthodique des sous-hommes" (<u>HR</u>: 485). And so the first is the <u>real</u> preference of Camus as well, what Lévy defines as "a morality of courage and duty confronting the dismal cowardice of submission to facts"[6]; and it is the subject of the two studies in the present essay.

The first of these studies _does_ claim for Camus, then, what that of Isaiah Berlin claims for Tolstoy, that his "was the spirit of empirical _inquiry_ which animated the great anti-theological and anti-metaphysical thinkers of the eighteenth century," and that his "realism and inability to be taken in by shadows made him their natural disciple."[7] And it is here that I disagree with Lévy, who asserts that most of these thinkers were the ancestors of the men to whom Camus was so steadfastly opposed, the "murderers of souls and torturers of bodies" whose spirit is "pure fidelity . . . to excess, to the idea of progress as it was thought out in the Enlightenment."[8] But it was Camus himself who carefully distinguished the moderate wing of that movement from its extremists and their descendants when he wrote in L'Homme Révolté that "les révoltes serviles, les révolutions régicides et celles du XXe siècle, ont . . . accepté, consciemment, une culpabilité de plus en plus grande dans la mesure où elles se proposaient d'instaurer une libération de plus en plus totale. Cette contradiction, devenue éclatante, empêche nos révolutionnaires d'avoir l'air de bonheur et d'espérance qui éclatait sur le visage et dans les discours de nos Constituants" (HR: 515). The latter, then, might well have said of their revolt what Camus did say of its modern version: "Elle prend le parti d'une limite où s'établit la communauté des hommes" (<u>HR</u>: 693). Like that of Camus, it was not one of excess, but of <u>mesure</u>, not one of faith in "historical," but in <u>human</u> reason.[9] And it was animated by the same critical spirit, the spirit of its philosophical allies, of Voltaire and Montesquieu, of Kant, and even of Rousseau, of those whom we may include among the <u>moderates</u> of the Enlightenment. Their universe, like that of Camus, "est celui du relatif" (<u>HR</u>: 693).

And yet as he well knew, and as I show in the second study of this essay, it is but one step from their "disenchanted" view of it to that of its <u>absurdity</u>, a view which most of them had not fully accepted, but whose moral consequences had already been drawn by some of the extremists to whom they were opposed. "Historiquement," writes Camus in <u>L'Homme Révolté</u>, "la première offensive cohérente est celle de Sade, qui rassemble en une seule et énorme machine de guerre les arguments de la pensée libertine jusqu'au curé Meslier et Voltaire. Sa négation est aussi, cela va de soi, la plus extrême. De la révolte, Sade ne tire que le non absolu" (<u>HR</u>: 447). Sade was a progenitor, then, of that nihilism which in despair of the world and of man as a part of it seeks refuge in their "transformation" through history. "Deux siècles à l'avance, sur une échelle réduite," says Camus, "Sade a exalté les sociétés totalitaires au nom de la liberté frénétique que la révolte en réalité ne réclame pas. Avec lui commencent réellement l'histoire et la tragédie contemporaines" (<u>HR</u>: 457).

And so if unlike most of his own predecessors Camus <u>does</u> fully accept the world's absurdity he also <u>rejects</u> the moral consequences which some of their enemies drew from it as a far <u>greater</u> evasion, as a flight from reality that has become a negation of the world and of man as its only end, but the very end in whom Camus reaffirms the faith of his ancestors against the descendants of those who opposed them.[10]

Notes

¹Bernard-Henri Lévy, *Barbarism with a Human Face*, trans. George Holoch (New York: Harper & Row, 1979), pp. 196-197.

²*Ibid.*, p. 197.

³*Ibid.*

⁴*Ibid.*

⁵*Ibid.*

⁶*Ibid.*

⁷Isaiah Berlin, *The Hedgehog and the Fox: An Essay on Tolstoy's View of History*, Touchstone Books (New York: Simon and Schuster, 1953), p. 11. Our italics.

⁸Lévy, *op. cit.*, p. 126. See also p. 175.

⁹Ernst Cassirer observes that "in the eighteenth century a pragmatic conception of history still prevails. No new critical concept appeared prior to the beginning of the nineteenth century, prior to the advent of Niebuhr and Ranke. From this time on, however, the modern concept of history is firmly established and it extends its influence over all the fields of human knowledge and human culture" (*An Essay On Man: An Introduction to a Philosophy of Human Culture* [New Haven: Yale Univ. Press, 1944], p. 192).

¹⁰Cf. Lester G. Crocker, *An Age of Crisis: Man and World in Eighteenth Century French Thought*, The Goucher College Series (Baltimore: The Johns Hopkins Press, 1959), pp. 472, 473: "The liberals and rationalists of our own time--the true children of the *philosophes*--still hope for a reasonable and a secular solution to the problems of the individual and society. They are beset, more critically than before, by the . . . forces which were their enemies in the eighteenth century crisis. . . . Embracing the nihilism, the philosophy of the absurd that was one child of the Enlightenment, [these forces] rebel against rationalism and objective standards, in the arts and in politics, in law and in morals, drift in aimless despair, in the liberal West, or follow some philosophy of naked power and amoral scientism. . . . [But] other men will go on, . . . and continue to strive for a rational, humane way of life." Albert Camus was among them.

O mon âme, n'aspire pas à la vie immortelle,
mais épuise le champ du possible.
> --Pindar, Pythian iii;
> epigraph to Le Mythe
> de Sisyphe

O homme! resserre ton existence au dedans de toi, et tu ne seras plus misérable. Reste à la place que la nature t'assigne dans la chaîne des êtres, rien ne t'en pourra faire sortir. . . . L'homme est très fort quand il se contente d'être ce qu'il est; il est très faible quand il veut s'élever au-dessus de l'humanité. N'allez donc pas vous figurer qu'en étendant vos facultés vous étendez vos forces; vous les diminuez, au contraire, si votre orgueil s'étend plus qu'elles.
> --Rousseau, Emile ou de l'éducation

Vie latine qui connaît ses limites,
Rassurant passé, oh! Méditerranée!
Encore sur tes bords des voix triomphent qui se sont tues,
    Mais qui affirment parce qu'elles t'ont niée!
> --Camus, "Poème sur la Méditerranée"

CHAPTER I

CAMUS AND THE ENLIGHTENMENT:
HIS PRAGMATIC RATIONALISM

"In the Springtime," writes Spengler in <u>The De-</u> <u>cline</u> <u>of</u> <u>the</u> <u>West</u>, "men could say '<u>Credo</u> <u>quia</u> <u>absur-</u> <u>dum</u>,' because they were certain that the comprehensible and the incomprehensible were <u>both</u> necessary constituents of the world--the nature which Giotto painted, in which the Mystics immersed themselves, and into which reason can penetrate, but only so far as the deity permits it to penetrate. But now [i.e., in the Age of Enlightenment and its aftermath] a secret jealousy breeds the notion of the Irrational--that which, as incomprehensible, is <u>therefore</u> valueless. It may be scorned openly as superstition, or privily as metaphysic. Only critically-established understanding possesses value."[1] But in <u>The</u> <u>Philosophy</u> <u>of</u> <u>the</u> <u>Enlightenment</u>, Spengler's Kantian contemporary Ernst Cassirer observes that before this critical understanding "the clear-cut form of the classical and medieval conception of the world crumbles, and the world <u>ceases</u> to be a 'cosmos' <u>in</u> <u>the</u> <u>sense</u> <u>of</u> <u>an</u> <u>immediately</u> <u>accessible</u> <u>order</u> <u>of</u> <u>things.</u>"[2]

This order disappears along with its Creator, hence reason as traditionally conceived is no longer "permitted" to penetrate anything, but is replaced by critical understanding. But there is a more radical version of this view which is not only held by philosophers who, like Cassirer, are sympathetic to the Enlightenment,[3] but also by several of those who, like Spengler, are among its most notable critics,[4] including Hegel himself. In his article on "Faith and Knowledge," for example, he fully concedes that during the movement's earliest phase "it was considered the death of philosophy if reason were to renounce its being in the absolute, simply excluding itself altogether from it and adopting a merely negative attitude toward it; but now," he adds, "just this became the highest point of philosophy."[5] Then, too, this later phase had already been implicit in the first, as the reason of the initially optimistic lumières was only "absolute" in their unqualified critique of a theistic and hence uncritically rational cosmology. Thus deprived of any divine light, it could not but become relative in their subsequent elaboration of a new system. If more scientific, this system was also less distinctly defined and hence incomplete, for the metaphysical darkness to which the reason had given rise now limited the extent of its knowledge to the realm of immediate phenomena:

> The negative procedure of the Enlightenment, whose positive side was . . . without any kernel, obtained a kernel by grasping its own negativity and by liberating itself from shallowness by means of the purity and infinity of the negative. On the other hand, the objects of its positive knowledge could therefore be merely finite and empirical things, while the eternal had to remain beyond. For knowledge, the eternal thus remains empty, [it is the] infinite empty space of knowledge. . . .[6]

And it is perhaps only in this tragic yet heroic sense, and not in Spengler's, that "Rationalism," as he has defined it, "signifies the belief in the data of critical understanding (that is, of the 'reason') alone."[7] For as another Kantian scholar, K. R. Popper, has stated, it is fundamentally "pragmatic," as far removed from what it calls uncritical rationalism as it is from irrationalism, since it affirms that "the 'world' is not rational, but [that] it is the task of science to rationalize it" (our italics):

> . . . an uncritical rationalism may argue that the world is rational and that the task of science is to discover this rationality, while an irrationalist may insist that the world, being fundamentally irrational, should be experienced and exhausted by our emotions and passions (or by our intellectual intuition) rather than by scientific methods. As opposed to this, pragmatic rationalism may recognize that the world is not rational, but demand that we submit or subject it to reason, as far as possible. Using Carnap's words . . . one could describe what I call "pragmatic rationalism" as "the attitude which strives for clarity everywhere but recognizes the never fully understandable or never fully rational entanglement of the

events of life".8

There are those, then, who unlike Spengler think rather of the essential modesty of the Enlightenment and its descendants than of their arrogance,9 of a moderation equidistant from the extremes of both his apparent obscurantism and the intellectual hubris which it pretends to condemn.10 Seemingly replying to Spengler in his philosophical essay, Le Mythe de Sisyphe, Albert Camus emerges as an exponent of pragmatic rationalism and exemplifies its spirit of temperance in an otherwise intemperate age:

> Il y a toujours eu des hommes pour défendre les droits de l'irrationnel. La tradition de ce qu'on peut appeler la pensée humiliée n'a jamais cessé d'être vivante. La critique du rationalisme a été faite tant de fois qu'il semble qu'elle ne soit plus à faire. Pourtant notre époque voit renaître ces systèmes paradoxaux qui s'ingénient à faire trébucher la raison comme si vraiment elle avait toujours marché de l'avant. Mais cela n'est point tant une preuve de l'efficacité de la raison que de la vivacité de ses espoirs. . . .
> Mais jamais peut-être [aussi] en aucun temps comme le nôtre, l'attaque contre la raison n'a été plus vive. (MS: 114)11

Hence reason is not omnipotent, and yet if it is not, then neither can it be "proven" to be ineffectual, for to attempt such a proof (as Spengler appears to have done elsewhere in his book12) is to deny as well the power of the reasoning employed in its formulation.

Absurdly, reason would then by its own powers be "proving" itself to be powerless. And yet it is true--as one of Camus's masters, Pascal, observed--that from one point of view "there is nothing so conformable to reason as this disavowal of reason."[13] Thus the disciple's rationalist sense of fairness would doubtless have granted that the systematic critique of rationalism in The Decline of the West was partly justified, and that as the author of L'Homme Révolté he might well have written of Spengler what he wrote of Hegel, Spengler's rationalistic counterpart: "Il y a dans Hegel, comme dans toute grande pensée, de quoi corriger Hegel" (HR: 543).[14] Hence there exists in this irrationalist critic of rationalism precisely that rationalist method which he criticizes but which contradicts his irrationalism. Yet he was nonetheless only partly justified in his criticism, for as Camus said of Hegel that he "rationalized to the point of being irrational" (HR: 541),[15] so one may say of Spengler that he "irrationalized" to the point of being rigidly rational, an assertion to whose truth one can easily attest after a close reading of both Form and Actuality and Perspectives of World-History. Each of the two volumes reveals a philosophy of pure historicism, or "the view that the history of anything is a sufficient explanation of it, that the values of anything can be accounted for

through the discovery of its origins, that the nature
of anything is entirely comprehended in its development, as for example, that the properties of the oak
tree are entirely accounted for by an exhaustive description of its development from the acorn."[16] But
"anything" includes even reason as a product of history, and Spengler proceeds in all "logic" to deny the
autonomy and hence the validity of all its forms except
the historical, which is by definition an <u>absolute</u>.[17]
He therefore believes philosophy to be synonymous with
hermeneutics, an activity of continual interpretation
due to the changeability of its reason[18]; for him it
becomes nothing more than <u>the history of its successive
stages of development</u>, and in the <u>Carnets</u> Camus aptly
summarizes the conclusion of his thought: "Ainsi
faisons-nous de <u>l'Histoire</u> de la Philosophie <u>l'unique
thème sérieux</u> de <u>toute</u> philosophie" (<u>CI</u>: 101).[19] Thus,
rigid rationality cannot in turn but culminate in <u>more</u>
irrationalism, and it is here that Spengler rejoins his
predecessor and where their systems converge[20]: extreme conformity to reason ultimately destroys it, and
there is nothing so conformable to it in its absolute
sense as a disavowal of it in its <u>relative and true</u>
sense. However, Camus also believed the inverse, or in
what constitutes the deeper meaning of Pascal's paradoxical maxim, that there is nothing more conformable

to reason in its relative and true sense than a disavowal of reason as an absolute[21]:

> On voit encore, on ne saurait trop y insister, que le rationalisme absolu n'est pas le rationalisme. Entre les deux, la différence est la même qu'entre cynisme et réalisme. Le premier pousse le second hors des limites qui lui donnent un sens et une légitimité. . . . C'est la violence en face de la force. (HR: 692)

Thus reason is not all, but if it is not, then neither is it nothing; it is neither all nor nothing, but something which Camus calls "mesure" in both thought and action, for "cynicism as a political attitude is only logical as a function of absolutist thought" (HR: 692).[22] The present spectacle of a world submerged in "the savage, formless movement of history" (HR: 704)[23] was born of the irrational belief that history is "exclusively" rational, that men cease to have any meaning when considered apart from it, that they are but unwitting agents in the process of its reason's ultimate self-realization.[24] Against this view, however, Camus reaffirms the rationalist faith in man as the measure of all things and in human rationality as that which alone is inherently conscious of its limits, and so he calls for a return to ethics and the pragmatic sense:

> La révolution du XXe siècle décrète que les valeurs sont mêlées au mouvement de l'histoire et sa raison historique justifie une nouvelle mystification. La mesure, face à ce

> dérèglement, nous apprend . . . qu'il faut une part de morale à tout réalisme: le cynisme est meurtrier. . . . (HR: 699-700)
>   L'important n'est donc pas encore de remonter à la racine des choses, mais, le monde étant ce qu'il est, de savoir comment s'y conduire. (HR: 414)25

Camus's entire thought is distinguished by such moderation, and we believe with Emmanuel Mounier that though it is unmistakably "contemporary" from the point of view of its content, namely the absurdity of the human condition, it is no less novel in its revival of the method which it applies to this content, namely that of the critical spirit which the lumières and Aufklärer brought to bear upon the irrationality of their own time[26]:

> [Camus] . . . applique l'épreuve inattendue de l'esprit de clarté sur l'horreur nocturne, la composition surprenante d'un Voltaire qui aurait lu Nietzsche et Jaspers en même temps que Descartes. . . . Il refuse l'harmonie qui disperse le drame, et il refuse la nuit, "cette nuit qui naît sous les yeux fermés et par la seule volonté de l'homme, nuit sombre et close que l'esprit suscite pour s'y perdre". A vouloir toutes les consolations de la clarté, l'homme divinise sa raison; à concevoir un monde trop irrationnel, il se jette, impuissant, à la divinité. De chaque côté il délire, et fuit sa condition dans le délire. . . . [Camus] nous reproche, somme toute, à trop chercher "le sens profond des choses", de ne savoir plus voir les choses. "Le monde n'est ni aussi rationnel, ni à ce point irrationnel. Il est déraisonnable, et il n'est que cela".
>   Tel est le premier climat, alors tout nouveau, de cette oeuvre: un rationalisme de l'irrationnel, une philosophie sombre des lumières.[27]

If he refuses harmony, it is because he also refuses the darkness, the incomprehensible which inevitably transforms and assimilates it. "Le thème de l'irrationnel," he states in Le Mythe de Sisyphe, "c'est la raison qui se brouille et se délivre en se niant" (MS: 134). But this is not to say that for Camus the negativity of the incomprehensible implies its "valuelessness," for he considers that the very enormity of its danger acts as a deterrent against the human propensity for "all the consolations of clarity" which paradoxically _result_ in it. "L'irrationnel limite le rationnel qui lui donne à son tour sa mesure" (HR: 699), runs the dictum of L'Homme Révolté[28]; "ceux qui s[e] . . . lancent [dans l'histoire] en prêchant sa rationalité absolue rencontrent servitude et terreur, et débouchent dans l'univers concentrationnaire" (HR: 648).[29] "Il y a [donc] des imbécillités," says Camus quoting Montesquieu, "qui sont telles qu'une plus grande imbécillité vaudrait mieux" (CII: 28).[30] Thus to deify reason is ultimately to deify that which is inimical to its continued preservation, for it is solely within its very _limits_ that it is to be preserved. "Si je reconnais les limites de la raison," writes Camus in Le Mythe, "je ne la nie pas pour autant, _reconnaissant ses pouvoirs relatifs_. Je veux seulement me tenir dans ce chemin moyen où l'intelligence peut rester claire" (MS:

127).³¹ For him the "ground" of this middle road can be none other than that of experience: "[La raison] a son ordre dans lequel elle est efficace. C'est justement celui de l'expérience humaine" (<u>MS</u>: 124-125). And it is here that Camus especially recalls Kant³² and his reference in the <u>Critique of Pure Reason</u> to the destruction of "all the ambitious attempts of reason to penetrate beyond the limits of experience."³³ Like Camus, Kant argues that the bounds of experience alone define those of the reason,³⁴ and that only they maintain the "life" of reason.³⁵ Both perceive that man is confined to a world whose limits so minimize the power of his reason to penetrate it that he is tempted in his natural desire for clarity to deny his own nature through an irrational or an uncritically rational nihilism. But they contend that acceptance of these limits is the only rational alternative to nihilism,³⁶ that through the very encounter between reason and the world which we call experience man is at least able to <u>order</u> the world and his life within it. In the words of K. R. Popper, a <u>pragmatic</u> rationalism "may recognize that the world is not rational, but demand <u>that we submit or subject it to reason</u>, as far as possible."³⁷ This is the message of Camus in <u>Le Mythe de Sisyphe</u>:

>Il est vain [aussi] de nier absolument la raison. . . . C'est pourquoi nous voulons tout rendre clair. Si nous ne le pouvons

> pas, . . . c'est justement à la rencontre de
> cette raison efficace mais limitée et de
> l'irrationnel toujours renaissant. . . .
> [L'homme raisonnable] reconnaît la lutte,
> [il] ne méprise pas absolument la raison et
> [il] admet l'irrationnel. Il recouvre ainsi
> du regard toutes les données de l'expérience
> et il est peu disposé à sauter avant de sa-
> voir. (MS: 124, 125)38

But to yield to the temptation, to overstep the bounds of experience in either direction is, as Mounier has it, to "flee from one's condition into a state of delirium." "On s'étonnerait en vain," asserts Camus, "du paradoxe apparent qui mène la pensée à sa propre négation par les voies opposées de la raison humiliée et de la raison triomphante. . . . C'est qu'en vérité le chemin importe peu, la volonté d'arriver suffit à tout. Le philosophe abstrait et le philosophe religieux partent du même désarroi et se soutiennent dans la même angoisse" (MS: 133).39 For Camus the only option is mesure, "the endless opposition of moderation to excess which has animated the history of the Occident since the time of the ancient world" (HR: 702).40

Notes

[1] Oswald Spengler, *Perspectives of World-History*, Vol. II of *The Decline of the West*, trans. Charles Francis Atkinson, Borzoi Books (New York: Alfred A. Knopf, 1928), p. 305. "And secrets," he continues, "are merely evidences of ignorance." See also p. 306: "Formerly philosophy was the handmaid of transcendent religiousness, but now . . . philosophy must . . . become scientific as epistemology and critique of nature and critique of values."

[2] Ernst Cassirer, *The Philosophy of the Enlightenment*, trans. Fritz C. A. Koelln and James P. Pettegrove (Princeton: Princeton Univ. Press, 1951), p. 37. Our italics. "Space and time," he writes, "are extended indefinitely; they can no longer be comprehended within that clearly defined scheme which classical cosmology possessed in Plato's doctrine of the five regular heavenly bodies or in Aristotle's hierarchical cosmos, nor can they be represented by finite measures and numbers" (*loc. cit.*). Cassirer agrees with Spengler that in what the latter calls the Springtime of the West, "reason is and remains the servant of revelation" (p. 40; cf. Spengler, *supra*, n. 1), but he points out that it is perfectible precisely insofar as it does remain so, since "the real perfection of nature is not to be found in nature itself but must be sought beyond the natural sphere. Neither science nor morality, neither law nor state, can be erected on its own foundations. Supernatural assistance is always needed to bring them to true perfection" (*loc. cit.*).

[3] See, for example, Jean A. Perkins, *The Concept of the Self in the French Enlightenment*, Histoire des Idées et Critique Littéraire, 94 (Geneva: Droz, 1969); and Harry Prosch, *The Genesis of Twentieth Century Philosophy: The Evolution of Thought from Copernicus to the Present*, Apollo Editions, 296 (New York: Thomas Y. Crowell, 1964). Perkins, an historian of ideas, similarly but more sharply contrasts the Scholastic approach to reality with that of the *philosophes*, stressing the influence on the latter of "Cartesian physics with its division of the universe into two substances" (p. 12). "Knowledge of material things, according to the Thomistic view," she states, "involves a participation on the part of the knower in the essential form of the known. It is this form which is transmitted in a rather mysterious way through the senses to the intellect. . . . [But] forms which g[i]ve being to matter [are] [now] no longer an acceptable explanation of phe-

nomena. . . . [For] in the Cartesian theory of perception there is no real interaction possible between the knower and the known, since they consist of totally unlike substances, mind and matter. This had not presented a problem to the Scholastics since each individual entity participated in both matter and form, and, therefore, there was no hard and fast break between the rational subject and the material object" (pp. 12, 16). Thus if the writers of the Enlightenment were indeed "striving to break out of the restrictive categories of past thought," they nonetheless "found the going very difficult. Those few who succeeded did so at the expense of considerable personal anguish" (p. 149). No such anguish, says Harry Prosch, is reflected in medieval man's view of things (op. cit., pp. 9, 20), a view in the very restrictiveness of whose categories "they acquired something like personal relations to him, since, like himself, they all did, somehow, pursue purposes. Nothing in nature, therefore, was totally dead, inert, or meaningless" (p. 10; see Chap. i, "The Copernican Revolution," pp. 9-21, passim).

[4]See, for example, William Barrett, *Irrational Man: A Study in Existential Philosophy*, Anchor Books, 321 (Garden City, N.Y.: Doubleday, 1958); Lucien Goldmann, *Le Dieu caché: Etude sur la vision tragique dans les Pensées de Pascal et dans le théâtre de Racine*, Coll. "Bibliothèque des Idées" (Paris: Gallimard, 1959); and Lester G. Crocker, *An Age of Crisis: Man and World in Eighteenth Century French Thought*, The Goucher College Series (Baltimore: The Johns Hopkins Press, 1959). If unlike Perkins and Prosch (see supra, n. 3) the Existentialist Barrett believes that "the ideology of the Enlightenment is thin, abstract, and therefore dangerous" (p. 275), he is at the same time far more emphatic than they in rejecting the simplistic view that "the passage from the Middle Ages to modern times is the substitution of a rational for a religious outlook" (p. 26). He asserts that "on the contrary, the whole of medieval philosophy--as Whitehead has very aptly remarked--is one of 'unbounded rationalism' in comparison with modern thought. Certainly," he observes, "the difference between a St. Thomas Aquinas in the thirteenth century and a Kant at the end of the eighteenth century is conclusive on this point: For Aquinas the whole natural world, and particularly this natural world as it opens toward God as First Cause, was transparently accessible to human reason; while to Kant, writing at the bitter end of the century of Enlightenment, the limits of human reason had very radically shrunk. (Indeed, . . . the very meaning of human reason became altered in Kant.) . . . The rationalism

of the medieval philosophers was contained by the mysteries of faith and dogma, which were altogether beyond the grasp of human reason, but were nevertheless powerfully real and meaningful to man as symbols that kept the vital circuit open between reason and emotion, between the rational and non-rational in the human psyche. Hence, this rationalism of the medieval philosophers does not end with the attenuated, bleak, or grim picture of man we find in the modern rationalists" (pp. 26-27; cf. pp. 24-25; for a differing view, see Peter Gay, The Enlightenment, An Interpretation: The Rise of Modern Paganism, The Norton Library, 870 [New York: W. W. Norton, 1977], Chap. iv, "The Retreat from Reason," pp. 207-255). Though Goldmann is a Marxist, and Crocker a "conservative" critic of the Enlightenment, both agree with Barrett and share in a similar view of Alexandre Koyré, himself an Existentialist and author of From the Closed World to the Infinite Universe (1957). "L'édifice thomiste avec la subordination de la philosophie à la théologie, de la raison à la foi, la physique aristotélicienne avec sa subordination du monde sublunaire au monde céleste," writes Goldmann, "seront renversés pour faire place à l'univers moniste et panthéiste de la philosophie de la nature. Mais comme le remarque à juste titre M. Koyré, la philosophie de la nature, en renversant le thomisme, n'avait pas mis à sa place un autre ordre précis et stable. Elle avait supprimé l'intervention miraculeuse de la divinité en l'intégrant au monde naturel. Mais par cette suppression du surnaturel, la nature avait perdu ses droits, et tout devenait à la fois naturel et possible. Le critère qui permettait de séparer l'erreur de la vérité, le témoignage de la fable, le possible de l'absurde s'estompait. . . . sur le plan physique, [le rationalisme] détruit l'idée d'univers ordonné, la remplaçant par celle d'un espace indéfini sans limites, ni qualités, et dont les parties sont rigoureusement identiques et interchangeables" (op. cit., pp. 36, 41). Cf. Crocker, op. cit., pp. 4, 5: "The challenge to the inherited order was complete and critical. . . . 'Man,' writes Alexandre Koyré, 'lost his place in the world, or more correctly perhaps, lost the very world in which he was living and about which he was thinking, and had to transform and replace not only his fundamental concepts and attributes, but even the very framework of this thought.' A cosmos ordered according to a hierarchy of value was replaced by an indefinite universe in which all components 'are placed on the same level of being.' . . . The Christian edifice . . . rested on the firm cornerstone of God's existence . . . the existence of a God as Christianity conceived him-- the infuser of order, meaning and value throughout his creation. . . ."

⁵Quoted in Walter Kaufmann, <u>Hegel</u>: <u>A Reinterpretation</u>, Anchor Books, 528a (Garden City, N.Y.: Doubleday, 1966), pp. 75-76. Our italics. (Significant portions of this otherwise inaccessible article are translated with valuable commentary in Chap. ii, Sec. 20 of Kaufmann's study, pp. 73-78.)

⁶<u>Ibid</u>., p. 75. Spengler, however, states that "[the] enlightened waking-consciousness . . . , under the guidance of the critical understanding, looks about it in a godless light-world and, when sense-perceptions are found not to square with sound human reason, treats sense as a 'lying jade'" (<u>op</u>. <u>cit</u>., p. 306). Thus, just as Christianity had subordinated reason to faith, the Enlightenment subordinates experience to reason, and this in "secret jealousy" (p. 305) of its predecessor. "The new <u>secretless</u> religion," he asserts, "is in its highest potentialities called wisdom (σοφία), its priests philosophers, and its adherents 'educated' people" (<u>loc</u>. <u>cit</u>.). But for Hegel the reverse is true, whence the basis for his own criticism of the Enlightenment: namely, that it subordinates reason to experience, and this to reason's <u>detriment</u>, for it is then reduced to "mere understanding" (<u>op</u>. <u>cit</u>., p. 75). "Nor did reason fail to develop some sense of its own inadequacy," comments Walter Kaufmann in summary of Hegel's argument; "its nemesis was that it excluded itself from the infinite, which had been the true goal of the religious spirit--and thus reason ended up, as it had done in the Middle Ages, as the handmaid of faith. . . . Kant already remarked that he had done away with knowledge to make room for faith, and in this respect he and Jacobi are at one. . . . The understanding, which is glued to the finite, sees divine images only as idols that have eyes and do not see, and the sacred grove only as so much wood. . . . Hegel opposes the philosophers who deny themselves the contemplation of the infinite and eternal, supposing that it dwells forever beyond reason; on the contrary, it is the task of reason and philosophy to contemplate the spirit in <u>this</u> world" (p. 77 [see Hegel's text, pp. 74-76, esp. p. 75]; cf. Karl Löwith, <u>From Hegel to Nietzsche</u>: <u>The Revolution in Nineteenth-Century Thought</u>, trans. David E. Green, Anchor Books, 553 [Garden City, N.Y.: Doubleday, 1967], pp. 304-305). In <u>L'Homme Révolté</u>, Camus himself contrasts the Hegelian God as World-Spirit with what he terms the mere "apparence de Dieu relégué dans le ciel des principes . . . [qui] sera le dieu de Kant, Jacobi et Fichte" (<u>HR</u>: 529). But he is as sharply critical of the one as he is of the

other, for the one inevitably fills the void created by the other, and this, he believes, with consequences which have proven disastrous for our time: "A la raison universelle, mais abstraite, . . . la pensée allemande a . . . fini par substituer une notion moins artificielle, mais aussi plus ambiguë, l'universel concret. . . . Dans la pensée fixe de son temps [elle] a [donc] introduit . . . un mouvement irrésistible. La vérité, la raison et la justice se sont brusquement incarnées dans le devenir du monde. . . . une grande partie de la démonstration hégélienne consiste à prouver que la conscience morale, dans sa banalité, celle qui obéit à la justice et à la vérité comme si ces valeurs existaient hors du monde, compromet, précisément, l'avènement de ces valeurs. La règle de l'action est donc devenue l'action elle-même qui doit se dérouler dans les ténèbres en attendant l'illumination finale. La raison, annexée par ce romantisme, n'est plus qu'une passion inflexible. . . . L'action n'est plus qu'un calcul en fonction des résultats, non des principes. . . . Avec . . . Hegel, philosophe napoléonien, commencent les temps de l'efficacité" (HR: 541, 542). These words, like those of William Barrett (see supra, n. 4), clearly reflect the view of one who is critical of the "ideology" of the Enlightenment. But they also reflect the view of one who persists in what Barrett calls the "practical task" of that movement: namely, criticism, and more specifically criticism of what is perceived to be "a social order . . . based everywhere on oppression, injustice, and even savagery" (op. cit., p. 275). For all our own reservations about the Enlightenment--and they are many--we do not accept Spengler's view that it completely subordinates experience to reason. (But neither are we unmindful of Professor Henri Peyre's contention that too much has been made of the role of experience in the thought of that century: "G. Lanson, dans une série d'articles qui ont ouvert la voie à des études fécondes," he writes, "a loué . . . le culte de l'expérience et la prudente sagesse réformatrice des Philosophes. Mais on a trop abondé dans ce sens. A mesure que s'éloignait la période héroïque de l'esprit philosophique, que minorité d'incroyants devenait majorité protégée par la Pompadour et Malesherbes, le siècle de Voltaire s'éprenait aussi de rhétorique creuse, de facile généralisation" [L'Influence des littératures antiques sur la littérature française moderne: Etat des travaux, Yale Romanic Studies, XIX (New Haven: Yale Univ. Press, 1941), p. 46; see Gustave Lanson, "Le Rôle de l'expérience dans la formation de la philosophie du XVIIIe siècle en France," in his Essais de méthode, de critique et d'histoire littéraire, ed. Henri Peyre (Paris: Hachette, 1965), pp.

297-335; and also Peyre's remarks on this article in his "Présentation," ibid., p. 19]).

⁷Spengler, op. cit., p. 305. We agree with Professor Henri Peyre (see supra, n. 6) that "certaine expérience manqua au XVIIIe siècle-- . . . et parfois le sens du grand et du tragique" (loc. cit.), but not with Ronald Grimsley that "the Enlightenment was never involved in a sense of the tragic" ("Preface," in From Montesquieu to Laclos: Studies on the French Enlightenment, Histoire des Idées et Critique Littéraire, 141 [Geneva: Droz, 1974], p. 1; our italics). Nor do we share Goldmann's similar view that "l'incompréhension radicale des rationalistes les plus pénétrants depuis Malebranche jusqu'à Voltaire et Valéry pour la position tragique est notoire, de même que celle des néo-kantiens pour l'esprit et la pensée kantienne" (op. cit., p. 35).

⁸Karl R. Popper, The High Tide of Prophecy: Hegel, Marx, and the Aftermath, Vol. II of The Open Society and Its Enemies, 5th ed., rev. (Princeton: Princeton Univ. Press, 1966), p. 357, n. 19. See also pp. 38, 213-214, 224, and 246. Cf. Immanuel Kant, Prolegomena to Any Future Metaphysics, ed. Lewis White Beck, The Library of Liberal Arts, 27 (Indianapolis: Bobbs-Merrill, 1950), p. 67: "The understanding does not derive its laws (a priori) from, but prescribes them to, nature" (Kant's italics). Goldmann (see supra, n. 7) would probably have been surprised to know that Popper is a Neo-Kantian.

⁹See Oswald Spengler, The Hour of Decision, Part One: Germany and World-Historical Evolution, trans. Charles Francis Atkinson, Borzoi Books (New York: Alfred A. Knopf, 1934), p. 9: "We are still in the Age of Rationalism, which began in the eighteenth century and is now rapidly nearing its close. . . . The word is familiar enough, but who knows how much it implies? It is the arrogance of the urban intellect. . . . It is the period in which everyone can read and write and therefore must have his say and always 'knows better.' This type of mind is obsessed by concepts--the new gods of the Age--and it exercises its wits on the world as it sees it." (See also supra, n. 6.) Compare this to Popper's important distinction between "true rationalism" and "pseudo-rationalism," op. cit., p. 227: "What I shall call the 'true rationalism' is the rationalism of Socrates. It is the awareness of one's limitations, the intellectual modesty of those who know how often they err. . . . It is the realization that we must not expect too much from reason; that argument rarely set-

tles a question, although it is the only means for learning--not to see clearly, but to see more clearly than before. What I shall call 'pseudo-rationalism' is the intellectual intuitionism of Plato. It is the immodest belief in one's superior intellectual gifts, the claim to be initiated, to know with certainty, and with authority. . . . This authoritarian intellectualism, this belief in the possession of an infallible instrument of discovery, or an infallible method, . . . this pseudo-rationalism is often called 'rationalism', but it is diametrically opposed to what we call by this name." And for Popper, it is *not* the "pseudo-rationalism" of Plato that the Enlightenment exemplifies, but the "true rationalism" of Socrates (see pp. 238-239 and p. 303, n. 61). Cf. also Peter Gay, who is kinder to Plato, but holds a similar view with respect to the intellectual kinship between Socrates and the philosophes (op. cit., pp. 81-82, 144). As opposed to "rationalism," however, Gay uses the term "criticism" to describe the philosophy of the Enlightenment. "The philosophes' glorification of criticism and their qualified repudiation of metaphysics," he explains, "make it obvious that the Enlightenment was not an Age of Reason but a Revolt against Rationalism. This revolt took two closely related forms: it rejected the assertion that reason is the sole, or even the dominant, spring of action; and it denied that all mysteries in the world can be penetrated by inquiry. The claim for the omnicompetence of criticism was in no way a claim for the omnipotence of reason" (p. 141; see Chap. iii, "The Climate of Criticism," pp. 127-203). In any case, it is clear that Gay's "criticism" is the equivalent of Popper's "pragmatic rationalism" (see supra, n. 8, and text).

[10]Cf. Peter Gay, who states that this moderation stemmed from what, "for the philosophes, was antiquity at its best, the source of its enduring power over them: hybris and credulity being routed by the spirit of criticism" (op. cit., p. 126). Cf. Voltaire: "Le philosophe n'est point enthousiaste, il ne s'érige point en prophète, il ne se dit point inspiré des dieux" (Dictionnaire philosophique, ed. Etiemble, Raymond Naves, and Julien Benda, Coll. "Classiques Garnier" [Paris: Garnier Frères, 1967], p. 342; art. "Philosophe").

[11]Our italics. Cf. Popper, op. cit., p. 229: "In the seventeenth, eighteenth, and nineteenth centuries, when the tide of rationalism, of intellectualism, and of 'materialism' was rising, irrationalists had to pay some attention to it, to argue against it; and by exhibiting its limitations, and exposing the immodest

claims and dangers of pseudo-rationalism (which they did not distinguish from rationalism in our sense), some of these critics, notably Burke, have earned the gratitude of all true rationalists. But the tide has now turned, and 'profoundly significant allusions . . . and allegories' (as Kant puts it) have become the fashion of the day." Like Popper, Camus read Spengler, and specifically referred to him in his Carnets (CI: 99-101).

12See, for example, Perspectives of World-History, p. 13: "For quite early, before he has begun to think abstractly, primitive man forms for himself a religious world-picture, and this is the object upon which the understanding begins to operate critically. Always science has grown up on a religion and under all the spiritual prepossessions of that religion, and always it signifies nothing more or less than an abstract melioration of these doctrines, considered as false because less abstract. Always it carries along the kernel of a religion in its ensemble of principles, problem-enunciations, and methods. Every new truth that the understanding finds is nothing but a critical judgment upon some other that was already there. The polarity between old and new knowledge involves the consequence that in the world of the understanding there is only the relatively correct--namely, judgments of greater convincingness than other judgments. Critical knowledge rests upon the belief that the understanding of to-day is better than that of yesterday. And that which forces us to this belief, is again, life." Thus for Spengler, "knowledge is only a late form of belief" (p. 271). (This conclusion is consistent with his own "belief"--doubtless of greater "convincingness" than others--that the Enlightenment is "secretly jealous" of Christianity. See the relevant passage cited, with our comments, supra, n. 6.)

13Blaise Pascal, Pensées, ed. Ch.-M. des Granges, Coll. "Classiques Garnier" (Paris: Garnier Frères, 1964), p. 146. Our translation of no. 272: "Il n'y a rien de si conforme à la raison que ce désaveu de la raison." Immediately following the longer passage cited in the previous note, Spengler asks the same question posed by Pascal before him, and answers it in the same way: "Can criticism . . . , as criticism, solve the great questions, or can it merely pose them? At the beginning of knowledge we believe the former. But the more we know, the more certain we become of the latter" (loc. cit.). And he even refers to "Bayle's profound observation that the understanding is capable only of discovering errors" (p. 13, n. 1). But this was what the philosophes themselves came to recognize as the consequence of their own procedure, Spengler's view to the contrary notwithstanding (see supra, n. 6, and especially the text to this note). "La philosophie de Voltaire," writes Raymond Naves, "repose . . . sur un relativisme lucide de la connaissance humaine, et on remarquera que dans cette partie critique, traditionnelle depuis l'Antiquité, elle ne diffère pas beaucoup de celle de Montaigne (ou de Pascal, qui prend tout à Montaigne pour cette démonstration)" ("Introduction," in Voltaire, Lettres philosophiques ou Lettres anglaises avec le texte complet des remarques sur les Pensées de Pascal, ed. Raymond Naves, Coll. "Classiques Garnier" [Paris: Garnier Frères, 1964], p. iv). Standing in this tradition is Albert Camus, for whom "Voltaire a soupçonné presque tout. Il n'a établi que très peu de choses, mais bien" (CII: 319). "Exception faite pour les rationalistes de profession," he writes in Le Mythe, "on désespère aujourd'hui de la vraie connaissance" (MS: 111). Voltaire says no less than this in praise of Locke and against the rationalists of the seventeenth century in his "Treizième lettre: Sur M. Locke": "Il vient enfin à considérer l'étendue ou plutôt le néant des connaissances humaines" (op. cit., p. 64; see also supra, n. 9). Cf. Patrick Henry, for whom "Albert Camus is quite easily linked with the long tradition of sceptical French thought from Montaigne to Voltaire and from Pascal to Vigny" (Voltaire and Camus: The Limits of Reason and the Awareness of Absurdity, Vol. CXXXVIII of Studies on Voltaire and the Eighteenth Century, ed. Theodore Besterman [Banbury, Eng.: The Voltaire Foundation, 1975], p. 59; see Chap. ii, "Camus," pp. 57-67, passim).

[14]See supra, n. 13. "Un esprit un peu rompu à la gymnastique de l'intelligence," observes Camus, "sait, comme Pascal, que toute erreur vient d'une exclusion. A la limite de l'intelligence on sait, de science certaine, qu'il y a du vrai dans toute théorie et qu'aucune des grandes expériences de l'humanité, même si apparemment elles sont très opposées, même si elles se nomment Socrate et Empédocle, Pascal et Sade, n'est a priori insignifiante" (CII: 78-79).

[15]Albert Camus, The Rebel: An Essay on Man in Revolt, trans. Anthony Bower, Vintage Books, 30 (New York: Random House, 1956), p. 133. Our italics. "Hegel a rationalisé jusqu'à l'irrationnel." See supra, n. 6.

[16]Dagobert D. Runes, ed., Dictionary of Philosophy (Totowa, N.J.: Littlefield, Adams, 1962), p. 127.

(Art. "Historicism," by James K. Feibleman.) See, for example, Form and Actuality, Vol. I of The Decline of the West, trans. Charles Francis Atkinson, Borzoi Books (New York: Alfred A. Knopf, 1926), pp. 3, 5-6, 21-22, 25-26, 100-101, 104-105, et passim. For Spengler, world-history is the "world-as-history" (p. 25), it is "a picture of endless formations and transformations, of the marvellous waxing and waning of organic forms" (p. 22). "Cultures are organisms," he asserts, "and world-history is their collective biography" (p. 104). See also Perspectives of World-History, pp. 48-51, 165, 169-170, 181, 274, 329, 361, et passim.

[17] See Perspectives of World-History, p. 274: "If there were truths independent of the currents of being [i.e., of history], there could be no history of truths." (See p. 329, where Spengler says of history that "it is cosmic," that "it is being.")

[18] Thomas Molnar traces the origins of philosophical hermeneutics to the Enlightenment and especially to Kant. The latter, he claims, "opened the way in philosophy to the endless search for the nature of understanding. In itself, this is a philosophical undertaking, but the search was conducted with an all-important modification of the traditional approach to epistemology: the object of the search was no longer the human mind as it makes contact with what is not it, the object became the human mind as a product of history, that is changing, and thus also changing its relationship with the world. More than that: the world too had to be conceived as changing in its essence, since according to the Kantian statement understanding prescribes its laws to nature. Thus, at every epoch marked by the historical changes of the mind, the object of knowledge, the apprehended world, also undergoes a radical alteration. Philosophy becomes hermeneutics, a work of constant interpretation. . . . By-products of this view of philosophy are such influential theories as historicism and evolutionism which . . . assume the existence of a trans-speculative yet immanent substratum, an essence called 'history' or an essence called 'evolution.' Such a substratum is nothing stable, it is regarded as a flux, a tension, a futurity" ("Philosophical Disorder," The Intercollegiate Review, 11, No. 1 [Fall 1975], 25, 26). But K. R. Popper, who is as vigorously critical of historicism as Molnar, takes issue with the view that Kant is its precursor or that he is a forerunner of Hegel, as Molnar later implies (26). On the contrary, says Popper, "Kant believed that it was possible to discover the one true and unchanging categorical apparatus, which repre-

sents as it were the necessarily unchanging framework of our intellectual outfit, i.e. human 'reason'. This part of Kant's theory was given up by Hegel, who, as opposed to Kant, did not believe in the unity of mankind. He taught that man's intellectual outfit was constantly changing" (op. cit., p. 214; see also pp. 38-41, 394-395, and 308, n. 30, as well as The Spell of Plato, Vol. I of The Open Society and Its Enemies, 5th ed., rev. [Princeton: Princeton Univ. Press, 1966], p. 247, n. 4). (Cf. Camus's similar, but more critical view, with our comments, supra, n. 6. On the whole, however, we agree with Lev Braun that "Hegel, according to Camus, has discarded all fixed standards of thought and conduct, such as human rights, or the principles of the Enlightenment" [Witness of Decline: Albert Camus, Moralist of the Absurd (Rutherford, N.J.: Fairleigh Dickinson Univ. Press, 1974), p. 144].)

[19]Our italics. This was in fact written at a time when Camus was still attracted by some of Spengler's ideas. But later he openly attacked the conclusion to which they led, as in the essay "Le parti de la liberté: hommage à Salvador de Madariaga." "Malgré sa culture encyclopédique," he said in praise of the latter, "il ne croit pas, comme nos penseurs officiels, que la philosophie consiste à enseigner l'histoire de la philosophie, mais il sait apparemment qu'elle consiste à exercer sa pensée pour chercher en même temps que les secrets du monde les règles d'une conduite, à essayer de vivre, en un mot, ce que l'on pense, en même temps que l'on tâche à penser correctement sa vie et son temps" (ESS: 1803). And again in the Carnets he wrote that "l'historicité laisse sans explication le phénomène de la beauté, c'est-à-dire les rapports avec le monde (sentiment de la nature) et les êtres en tant qu'individus (amour)" (CII: 174).

[20]Cf. Judith N. Shklar, who says of Spengler that "he was ultimately closer to Hegel than to the latter's opponents" (After Utopia: The Decline of Political Faith [Princeton: Princeton Univ. Press, 1957], p. 79).

[21]"Pascal: L'erreur vient de l'exclusion" (CII: 58).

[22]Camus, op. cit., p. 289. "Le cynisme, comme attitude politique, n'est logique qu'en fonction d'une pensée absolutiste." Fixed at the meridian between the two poles of absolutist thought, "le nihilisme absolu d'une part, le rationalisme absolu de l'autre" (HR: 692), Camus's "mesure" is the equivalent of Popper's

"pragmatic rationalism" (see supra, nn. 8-11, and text). Maurice Cranston states that "there are points of resemblance between Camus' political thought and that of Sir Karl Popper who belongs to the Kantian liberal tradition. . . . There are many interesting parallels to be discerned between L'Homme Révolté and both The Open Society and The Poverty of Historicism of Popper. Philip Thody tells me that Camus possessed a copy of The Open Society" ("Albert Camus," Encounter, 28, No. 2 [Feb. 1967], 52, n. 14; see also Philip Thody, "Camus et la politique," Albert Camus 2: Langue et Langage, ed. Brian T. Fitch, La Revue des Lettres Modernes, Nos. 212-216 [1969], pp. 143-144). Compare Camus's critique of Hegel and Marx in L'Homme Révolté (HR: 541-555, 593-630) with that of Popper in The High Tide of Prophecy: Hegel, Marx, and the Aftermath, pp. 27-211, 304-351.

[23]Camus, op. cit., p. 301. "Le mouvement informe et furieux de l'histoire."

[24]"Il faut connaître les conclusions dernières de Feuerbach dans sa Théogonie pour apercevoir la source profondément nihiliste de ces pensées enflammées," writes Camus. "Contre Hegel lui-même, Feuerbach affirmera, en effet, que l'homme n'est que ce qu'il mange et il résumera ainsi sa pensée et l'avenir: 'La véritable philosophie est la négation de la philosophie. Nulle religion est ma religion. Nulle philosophie est ma philosophie.' Le cynisme, la divinisation de l'histoire et de la matière, la terreur individuelle ou le crime d'Etat, ces conséquences démesurées vont alors naître, toutes armées, d'une équivoque conception du monde qui remet à la seule histoire le soin de produire les valeurs et la vérité" (HR: 554).

[25]Our italics. Lev Braun correctly states that "in his appeal to Greek thought, Camus tends to leave out the intellectualistic tradition as represented by Aristotle and perhaps the late Plato and borrow from the pre-Socratic philosophers and poets. For these, reason was concerned with conduct rather than with epistemology. Reason meant measure, the respect for limits, and the practice of self-restraint. It was the opposite of hubris" (op. cit., p. 127). But the same may be said for Socrates, who, in the words of Peter Gay, "proclaimed the vanity of cosmology compared to the knowledge that leads men to right action. The philosophes had much sympathy with this point of view; it reappears . . . in their suspicion of metaphysics and in their commitment to practicality" (op. cit., pp. 81-82). And it reappears again in Camus: "C'est Socrate

qui a raison, contre Jésus et Nietzsche," he writes. "Le progrès et la grandeur vraie est dans le dialogue à hauteur d'homme et non dans l'évangile, monologué et dicté du haut d'une montagne solitaire. Voilà où j'en suis" (<u>CII</u>: 161-162).

26We therefore agree with Jean Sarocchi that "ce philosophe de l'absurde hérite de son atavisme latin une solide tradition de rationalité," but reject his view that Camus "défend les démons de la conscience d'une manière fort raisonnable" (<u>Camus</u>, Coll. "'SUP': Philosophes" [Paris: Presses Universitaires de France, 1968], p. 26).

27Emmanuel Mounier, "Albert Camus ou l'appel des humiliés," <u>Esprit</u>, 18, No. 1, <u>Les Carrefours de Camus</u> (Jan. 1950), 29. Our italics. Mounier's quotations are from <u>Le Mythe de Sisyphe</u>. See the <u>Essais</u> (<u>MS</u>: 146, 154, 134).

28On the other hand, "le rationalisme le plus universel finit toujours par buter sur l'irrationnel de la pensée humaine" (<u>MS</u>: 116).

29"Et le rationalisme le plus absolu que l'histoire ait connu," writes Camus of Marxism in the <u>Actuelles</u>, "finit, comme il est logique, par s'identifier au nihilisme le plus absolu" (<u>AI</u>: 361).

30Camus echoes Montesquieu in the following passage from his tribute to Madariaga: "L'intelligence sans caractère est bien pire, à la fin, que la très heureuse imbécillité. Faute de volonté ferme, elle se donne volontiers à une doctrine implacable et c'est ainsi qu'on a vu naître cette espèce si particulière à notre temps: l'intellectuel dur, prêt à justifier toutes les terreurs au nom du seul réalisme" (<u>ESS</u>: 1805).

31Our italics. "Si c'est là son orgueil," he adds, "je ne vois pas de raison suffisante pour y renoncer" (<u>MS</u>: 127).

32Patrick Henry's comparison with Voltaire is equally valid: "This notion of reason," he writes, "is similar to that of the Enlightenment in general and to that of Voltaire in particular in the sense that it is empirically oriented, anti-rationalist and <u>a posteriori</u>. Like Voltaire's, it emphasizes the shortcomings of reason and cries aloud for the use, not the abuse of reason" (<u>op. cit</u>., p. 105).

33Immanuel Kant, Critique of Pure Reason, trans. J. M. D. Meiklejohn, Everyman's Library, No. 1909 (London: J. M. Dent; New York: E. P. Dutton, 1934), p. 469. See also p. 397, where he explains that "it has then . . . ventured into the region of the incomprehensible and unsearchable, on the heights of which it loses its power and collectedness, because it has completely severed its connection with experience" (our italics).

34See Critique of Pure Reason, p. 434: "Reason is not to be considered as an indefinitely extended plane, of the bounds of which we have only a general knowledge; it ought rather to be compared to a sphere, the radius of which may be found from the curvature of its surface. . . . Beyond the sphere of experience there are no objects which it can cognize."

35The phrase is from John Herman Randall, Jr., From the German Enlightenment to the Age of Darwin, Vol. II of The Career of Philosophy (New York: Columbia Univ. Press, 1965), p. 157. See Critique of Pure Reason, pp. 15-16: "A cursory view of the present work will lead to the supposition that its use is merely negative, that it only serves to warn us against venturing, with speculative reason, beyond the limits of experience. This is, in fact, its primary use. But this, at once, assumes a positive value, when we observe that the principles with which speculative reason endeavours to transcend its limits, lead inevitably, not to the extension, but to the contraction of the use of reason, inasmuch as they threaten to extend the limits of sensibility, which is their proper sphere, over the entire realm of thought, and thus to supplant the pure (practical) use of reason. So far, then, as this criticism is occupied in confining speculative reason within its proper bounds, it is only negative; but, inasmuch as it thereby, at the same time, removes an obstacle which impedes and even threatens to destroy the use of practical reason, it possesses a positive and very important value. In order to admit this, we have only to be convinced that there is an absolutely necessary use of pure reason--the moral use--in which it inevitably transcends the limits of sensibility, without the aid of speculation, requiring only to be insured against the effects of a speculation which would involve it in contradiction with itself. To deny the positive advantage of the service which this criticism renders us, would be as absurd as to maintain that the system of police is productive of no positive benefit, since its main business is to prevent the violence which citizen has to apprehend from citizen, that so each may pursue his vocation in peace and security." Let us note here our agreement with Lev Braun that while Camus may be "a Kantian [without] practical reason" in the sense that he "firmly rejects any intimation of transcendence," it is nevertheless true that the cornerstone of his humanism "coincides with one of Kant's criteria of the ethical act, namely, that man should be regarded as end and not as means" (op. cit., pp. 133, 122; cf. supra, nn. 24-25, and text).

36Cf. Lev Braun, who holds that "at the time of totalitarian revolution and logical crime, Camus found himself--mutatis mutandis--in the same situation as Kant between the Marquis de Sade and the Terror" (op. cit., pp. 111-112).

37Karl R. Popper, The High Tide of Prophecy: Hegel, Marx, and the Aftermath, p. 357, n. 19. (See supra, n. 8, and text.)

38"Le Mythe est un livre de volonté," writes Mounier. "Kant y tient Ménalque en tutelle" (art. cit., 31).

39"Quant aux conséquences," he later observes, "il n'y a pas de différence entre les deux attitudes" (HR: 692).

40Camus, op. cit., p. 299. "La longue confrontation entre la mesure et la démesure qui anime l'histoire de l'Occident, depuis le monde antique." Camus's attitude corresponds to what Popper calls "the rationalist interpretation of history." This interpretation "views with hope those periods in which man attempted to look upon human affairs rationally. It sees in the Great Generation and especially in Socrates, in early Christianity (down to Constantine), in the Renaissance and the period of the Enlightenment, and in modern science, parts of an often interrupted movement, the efforts of men to free themselves, to break out of the cage of the closed society, and to form an open society. It is aware that this movement does not represent a 'law of progress' or anything of that sort, but that it depends solely upon ourselves, and must disappear if we do not defend it against its antagonists as well as against laziness and indolence" (The High Tide of Prophecy: Hegel, Marx, and the Aftermath, p. 303, n. 61).

[Or,] j'admire qu'on puisse trouver au bord de la Méditerranée des certitudes et des règles de vie, qu'on y satisfasse sa raison et qu'on y justifie un optimisme et un sens social. Car enfin, ce qui me frapp[e] [maintenant] ce n'[est] pas un monde fait à la mesure de l'homme--mais qui se referm[e] sur l'homme.
      --Camus, L'Envers et l'Endroit

Voués par position à l'optimisme, les humanistes ont senti chanceler leur foi . . . : certes, ils ne cèdent pas au vertige du chaos et de l'absurde, mais ils ont appris que, dans la marche des peuples, de graves accidents sont toujours possibles et des erreurs d'itinéraires toujours à craindre; et surtout, ils ont dû apprécier plus exactement l'importance et l'autonomie de certains facteurs . . . : l'épaisseur de la matière et du temps, le coefficient de résistance du monde humain au rationnel.
  --Pierre-Henri Simon, L'Esprit et l'Histoire: Essai sur la conscience historique dans la littérature du XXe siècle

Pour un esprit absurde la raison est vaine et il n'y a rien au-delà de la raison.
      --Camus, Le Mythe de Sisyphe

CHAPTER II

CAMUS AND EXISTENTIAL PHILOSOPHY:
HIS TRAGIC REALISM

We may observe with one critic, however, that while "Camus's view of life does not differ in substance from the views of the classical humanists of the Graeco-Roman and European traditions," it is far more tragic than theirs, for it was born in the metaphysical upheaval of the twentieth century, "at a time when values had to be defended at the price of life in a world that denies them."[1] The climate of contemporary nihilism is unlike any other in all the previous history of the West, as man is faced with an increasingly senseless order of things which he cannot accept and desperately tries to dispel in a relentless quest for their unity in some "profound" but elusive meaning. "Cette fièvre qui soulève le coeur au-dessus d'un monde éparpillé, dont il ne peut cependant se déprendre, est la fièvre de l'unité," writes Camus. "Elle ne débouche pas dans une médiocre évasion, mais dans la revendication la plus obstinée. Religion ou crime, tout effort humain obéit, finalement, à ce désir déraisonnable et prétend donner à la vie la forme qu'elle n'a pas" (HR: 666). The passion for coherence is intrinsic to man, transcending both time and place[2]; but it is now more intense than ever before, as he violently rebels against that new evidence of which he is himself a part, "ce divorce entre l'esprit qui désire et le monde qui déçoit, ma nostalgie d'unité, cet univers dispersé et la contradiction qui les enchaîne": "cette évidence," says Camus, "c'est l'absurde" (MS: 135).[3] It had not yet revealed itself in the Age of Criticism,[4] for most men of that time could still say with Montesquieu that "our soul is made for thinking, that is, for perceiving."[5] But as Kant was soon among the first to fully realize, man's very nature determines that his libido sciendi, his lust for knowledge, is to remain forever unsatisfied.[6] This is the way Kant expresses it in his first preface to the Critique of Pure Reason:

> Human reason, in one sphere of its cognition, is called upon to consider questions, which it cannot decline, as they are presented by its own nature, but which it cannot answer, as they transcend every faculty of the mind.
> It falls into this difficulty without any fault of its own. It begins with principles, which cannot be dispensed with in the field of experience, and the truth and sufficiency of which are, at the same time, insured by experience. With these principles it rises, in obedience to the laws of its own nature, to ever higher and more remote conditions. But it quickly discovers that, in this way, its labours must remain ever incomplete, because new questions never cease to present

> themselves; and thus it finds itself compelled to have recourse to principles which transcend the region of experience, while they are regarded by common sense without distrust. It thus falls into confusion and contradictions, from which it conjectures the presence of latent errors, which, however, it is unable to discover, because the principles it employs, transcending the limits of experience, cannot be tested by that criterion. The arena of these endless contests is called **Metaphysic**.[7]

Hence through no set of principles can we know the world "as it is in itself," that is, as it "is" beyond experience, and in this Camus thoroughly concurs: "Je comprends," he states in Le Mythe, "que, si je puis par la science saisir les phénomènes et les énumérer, je ne puis pour autant appréhender le monde" (MS: 112).[8]

Yet unlike Camus, and for all his own strictures against metaphysics, even Kant affirms the existence of the thing-in-itself[9] and thus poses the dualism of noumena and phenomena, of unknowable things in themselves and their "knowable" appearance in the objects of experience. These objects or phenomena, however, are therefore nothing but representations to human consciousness of that which they conceal. Thus they conform to the mind, whose reason, as a critical Jean-Paul Sartre has explained, "finds in things only what [it] [has] put into them."[10] And his description is quite accurate, for in the second preface to the Critique Kant himself states the critical philosophy's position on the cognitive function of reason in the following terms:

> . . . reason only perceives that which it produces after its own design; . . . it . . . must proceed in advance with principles of judgment according to unvarying laws, and compel nature to reply to its questions.
> . . . It is only the principles of reason which can give to concordant phenomena the validity of laws, and it is only when experiment is directed by these rational principles that it can have any real utility. Reason must approach nature with the view, indeed, of receiving information from it, not, however, in the character of a pupil, who listens to all that his master chooses to tell him, but in that of a judge, who compels the witnesses to reply to those questions which he himself thinks fit to propose. . . .
> . . . we only cognize in things a priori that which we ourselves place in them.[11]

Hence in terms of epistemology even Kant rationalizes to the point of being irrational,[12] for so <u>domesticating</u> the world that it nearly becomes a creation of the human mind, he borders on metaphysical solipsism, that "subvariety of <u>idealism</u> which maintains that the individual self of the solipsistic philosopher is the whole of reality and that the external world . . . [is] [a] representation of that self having no independent existence."[13] But then it is clear that whether wholly or even partially determined by man's intellect, the Kantian sphere of synthetic phenomena also serves to protect him from what he already perceives to be a hostile world whose forces are beyond the control of his reason, for it acts as a buffer between these forces and that of his self-destructive will to dissipate them. "Criticism alone," Kant himself writes, "can strike a blow at the root of Materialism, Fatalism, Atheism, Free-thinking, Fanaticism, and Superstition, which are universally injurious. . . . If governments think proper to interfere with the affairs of the learned, it would be more consistent with a wise regard for the interests of science, as well as for those of society, to favour a criticism of this kind, by which alone the labours of reason can be established on a firm basis."[14]

Yet while such mesure may have been more than adequate for the eighteenth century, it proves unequal to the demands of the nineteenth and twentieth, for with the advent in this period of that existential philosophy anticipated by Kant, the clear-cut form of his own conception of the world crumbles as well, and like the eternal which it had replaced, the protective screen of criticism fades into nothingness. Man, Camus tells us, is then at last confronted by the hostile world from which he had long been isolated:

> Un degré plus bas et voici l'étrangeté: s'apercevoir que le monde est "épais", entrevoir à quel point une pierre est étrangère, nous est irréductible, avec quelle intensité la nature, un paysage peut nous nier. . . . L'hostilité primitive du monde, à travers les millénaires, remonte vers nous. Pour une se-

> conde, nous ne le comprenons plus puisque
> pendant des siècles nous n'avons compris en
> lui que les figures et les dessins que préa-
> lablement nous y mettions, puisque désormais
> les forces nous manquent pour user de cet ar-
> tifice. Le monde nous échappe puisqu'il re-
> devient lui-même. Ces décors masqués par
> l'habitude redeviennent ce qu'ils sont. . . .
> Une seule chose: <u>cette épaisseur et cette
> étrangeté du monde, c'est l'absurde</u>. (<u>MS</u>:
> 107, 108)15

Here in <u>Le Mythe de Sisyphe</u> Camus concisely expresses what Sartre has already said in his novel, <u>La Nausée</u>,16 and is later to say more philosophically in his essay on phenomenological ontology, <u>L'Etre et le Néant</u>: this world ceases to depend in any way for its existence upon man's rational perception of it; it no longer "refers" to an in-itself,17 but rather reveals that it "<u>is</u> in-itself," that it "<u>is</u>" and "is what it is" (<u>EN</u>: 34),18 the massive <u>Being-in-itself</u> that "overflows the knowledge which [he] has of it" (<u>EN</u>: 16)19 and thus invades his consciousness:

> . . . c'est l'être même qui est présent à la
> conscience dans la connaissance et . . . le
> Pour-soi [i.e., consciousness] n'ajoute <u>rien</u>
> à l'En-soi, sinon le fait même <u>qu'il y ait</u> de
> l'En-soi. . . . le monde et la chose-usten-
> sile, l'espace et la quantité comme le temps
> universel [sont] de purs néants substantiali-
> sés et ne modifi[ent] en rien l'être pur qui
> se révèle à travers eux. En ce sens, tout
> est donné, tout est présent à moi sans dis-
> tance et dans son entière réalité; <u>rien</u> de ce
> que je vois ne vient de moi, il n'y a <u>rien</u> en
> dehors de ce que je vois ou de ce que <u>je</u>
> pourrais voir. L'être est partout autour de
> moi, il semble que je puisse le toucher, le
> saisir; la <u>représentation</u>, comme événement

> psychique, est une pure invention des philosophes. . . . l'être est partout, contre moi, autour de moi, il pèse sur moi, il m'assiège et je suis perpétuellement renvoyé d'être en être. (__EN__: 269, 270)[20]

For Sartre as for Camus, the real world's hostility to man is its revealed <u>resistance</u> against his every effort to reduce it to rational terms, to render it meaningful, and thereby find his <u>own</u> meaning within it. Eternally solid and <u>in</u>-itself, "the synthesis of itself with itself" (__EN__: 33),[21] the Being of the world is what man <u>is</u> <u>not</u> and can never be, but also what he <u>yearns</u> to be in order "to be" complete, for "in [his] coming into existence [he] grasps [himself] as an <u>in</u>complete being" (__EN__: 132),[22] as "a <u>lack</u> of being haunted in its inmost being by the being of which it is desire" (__EN__: 131).[23] Thus as each being is inherently inaccessible to him, he is "perpetually referred from being to being" in his quest for being; he is <u>for</u>-itself, or the <u>very</u> <u>longing</u> for unity which Kant had only said that he <u>felt</u>[24] but could not satisfy. Yet in this connection, Pascal--whom we have already mentioned with Kant[25]--is far more direct and dramatic, his <u>Pensées</u> proving to be the epistemological forerunner of both <u>Le</u> <u>Mythe</u> <u>de</u> <u>Sisyphe</u> and <u>L'Etre</u> <u>et</u> <u>le</u> <u>Néant</u>, when they read:

> Voilà notre état véritable. . . . Nous voguons sur un milieu vaste, toujours incertains et flottants, poussés d'un bout vers l'autre. Quelque terme où nous pensions nous

> attacher et nous affermir, il branle et nous
> quitte et si nous le suivons, il échappe à
> nos prises, nous glisse et fuit d'une fuite
> éternelle. Rien ne s'arrête pour nous.
> C'est l'état qui nous est naturel, et toute-
> fois le plus contraire à notre inclination;
> nous brûlons de désir de trouver une assiette
> ferme, et une dernière base constante pour y
> édifier une tour qui s'élève à l'infini; mais
> tout notre fondement craque, et la terre
> s'ouvre jusqu'aux abîmes.26

Hence man as the being "unsettled" in its being is <u>ra-
tional</u> man confronted by the <u>non</u>rational world, a world
to whose fullness he is naturally <u>attracted</u> in his passion for unity and yet one from which he is simultane-
ously <u>repelled</u> by this fullness, which it impenetrably
<u>is</u> and is forever what-he-<u>is-not</u>.27 His reason may
well have served to "protect" him from the world to the
extent that it superimposed itself "up-on" the world in
his effort to order it28; but now it is the source of
his vulnerability to its presence before him, for it is
no more than the very <u>lack</u> which he is in <u>pursuit</u> of
the world, a lack which in distinguishing itself as
conscious from what is eternally <u>non</u>conscious and yet
remaining ever <u>near</u> it is forever incapable both of
<u>grasping</u> it and hence of <u>preventing</u> it from "'invest-
[ing] [him]' on every side" (<u>EN</u>: 269).29 Thus as Pascal observes, we are "driven from end to end" of the
world <u>by</u> the world precisely inasmuch as at every point
"it eludes <u>our</u> grasp, slips past <u>us</u>, and flees from <u>us</u>
in eternal flight."30 This is what Sartre means when

he writes that "being is everywhere around _me_"; it therefore only "_seems_ that _I_ can touch it, grasp it": for "the world evades _us_," as Camus says, precisely "because it becomes _itself_ again," its hostility to us consisting in its inaccessibility to our _own_ _reason_ and to _ourselves_, whose own reason we _are_ in not being.

And so _as_ rational beings, as those who forever differentiate _themselves_ from being _as-not_ what being _is_, we only relate to and hence "order" being through what Sartre calls the _negation_ of being which _we_ are—that is, through the _external_ _differentiation_ of being which we effect as _nothing_ but _our-own_ differentiation _from_ being.[31] And yet if this is true, if the differentiation of being "from" ourselves _is_ in fact _nothing_-more than ourselves, then being cannot but be revealed-to-us-"through" ourselves in the form of that world-which-_we_-_perceive_ before us:

> Ainsi le sens même du pour-soi est dehors dans l'être, mais c'est par le pour-soi que le sens de l'être apparaît. Cette totalisation de l'être n'ajoute _rien_ à l'être, elle n'est rien que la manière dont l'être se dévoile comme n'étant pas le pour-soi, la manière dont _il y a_ de l'être; elle paraît _hors du pour-soi_, échappant à toute atteinte, comme ce qui détermine le pour-soi dans son être. . . . Mais, si le pour-soi doit être le néant par quoi "il y a" de l'être, il ne peut y avoir de l'être originellement que comme totalité. (_EN_: 230)

Thus we come to grasp the full meaning of Sartre's affirmation--and its importance as a statement reflecting the revolution in Western thought since Kant--"that it is being which is present to consciousness in knowledge and that the For-itself adds nothing to the In-itself, except the very fact that there is In-itself"32: epistemologically, rational man is no longer the being whom Kant had implicitly defined as the fashioner of a world which encloses and hence conceals being, but rather the being who is his own discovery of a world which is being as-he-sees-it. "Penser, ce n'est pas unifier, rendre familière l'apparence sous le visage d'un grand principe," asserts Camus in agreement with Husserl and thus with Sartre; "penser, c'est . . . diriger sa conscience, . . . [laquelle] ne forme pas l'objet de sa connaissance, [mais] fixe seulement, [car] elle est l'acte d'attention et, pour reprendre une image bergsonienne, elle ressemble à l'appareil de projection qui se fixe d'un coup sur une image. . . . C'est cette 'intention' qui caractérise la conscience. . . . C'est une façon d'éveiller un monde somnolent et de le rendre vivant à l'esprit" (MS: 129, 130, 131).33

And yet the phenomenological tradition which Camus shares not only with Sartre but with such pre-Husserlian thinkers as Kierkegaard34 and Nietzsche is no more than the inevitable outgrowth of an Enlightenment brought to the realization that if its critique of a theistic cosmology had once for all limited the extent of possible knowledge to the realm of immediate phenomena, then <u>one could never hope to apprehend any so-called</u> "<u>essence of being</u>"[35]--a conclusion which in its lattermost development marks the birth of that tradition as one of its principal tenets.[36] Thus if at first this inapproachability of being from the perspective of the modern consciousness was only "expressed" in terms of Kant's hidden thing-in-itself,[37] it is now the defining characteristic of that into which the thing-in-itself has been entirely "realized" and rendered superfluous in its role as mere concept: namely, the <u>Being</u>-in-itself of existential philosophy. This new version of in-itself is the in-itself-as-"being," which is to say that it is no less than Kant's <u>inapprehensible</u> being <u>made manifest</u> in concrete terms. And this is in no way a contradiction, for while the being of the object is now fully given in each of its appearances,[38] each appearance of the object reveals it in but one aspect of its being, so that the being of the object is the ever present but forever unrevealed totality-of-possible-aspects to which the object has been logically reduced from what Nietzsche called the mere "illusion" of the inaccessible "world-behind-the-scene" (<u>EN</u>: 12)[39]--a "world" all of whose other aspects are now accordingly, <u>yet undetectably</u> there when the object _as_ totality _appears_ in that aspect. "Ce qui paraît, en effet," observes Sartre, "c'est seulement un _aspect_ de l'objet et l'objet est tout entier _dans_ cet aspect et tout entier hors de lui. Tout entier _dedans_ en ce qu'il se manifeste _dans_ cet aspect: il s'indique lui-même comme la structure de l'apparition, qui est en même temps la raison de la série. Tout entier dehors, car la série elle-même n'apparaîtra jamais ni ne peut apparaître" (_EN_: 13).[40] Therefore, if at the same time that the object reveals itself to us as it is in _one_ aspect it _conceals_ itself from us as it is in _every_ _and_ _all_ _other_ aspects, the being of the _total_ _phenomenon_ which it is _cannot_ be reduced to any single, immediate phenomenon-of-its-"being" before us: "l'être des phé-nomènes," says Sartre of all objects in general, "ne se résoud pas en un phénomène d'être" (_EN_: 15). Thus if in its contemporary form the existent-as-totality is that which is _present_ to us as "no more" than the infinite series of individual appearances which manifest it,[41] it is nonetheless true of this existent that _as_ such a series it is an entity whose own being is as imperceptible _in_ _itself_ as the being of its Kantian forerunner.

But then if this is so, if the Being-in-itself itself does not reveal itself in-itself, it is precisely because, _unlike_ the thing-in-itself, it neither conceals itself in-itself, but does so only partially, and so only partially reveals itself. And indeed <u>self</u>-concealment cannot but <u>by definition</u> be partial, for in order that something should <u>completely</u> hide itself by means of itself, it would require no less than its <u>entire</u> self, so that its total concealment would necessarily imply its total revelation, which is absurd. Hence the thing-in-itself as that which conceals itself in-itself is but a meaningless concept; it has no basis whatsoever in fact, for fact is the reality that we <u>perceive</u> as what cannot in any way conceal <u>itself</u> without partially <u>revealing</u> itself in no less than one <u>profile</u> of itself[42]; and this it does by concealing itself in all others <u>alone,</u> the latter "making room" within itself, as it were, for the former's appearance <u>as</u> the <u>appearance-of-itself</u>.

Therefore, while the phenomenon of being is not the being of the phenomenon, it <u>is</u> nevertheless a <u>part</u> of that being, it is being as the latter conceals itself <u>by partially revealing itself</u> and <u>not</u>, as Kant implied, an "outside" of being belonging to being, yet so far removed from it as to serve as a screen behind which it "completely" conceals itself; for this is tantamount to saying that being hides itself behind <u>itself</u>, a clear violation of the law of contradiction. It follows, then, that the Being-in-itself cannot be "totally" concealed but by something _other_ than itself, by other Beings-in-themselves or by things other than being. The Kantian phenomenon may be said to fall into the second category, for it is largely a creation of the _non_-being of man's consciousness, a _fixed representation_ invented by human reason.⁴³ The "appearance" of rationality was thus a mask that is now lifted, and the being it concealed is no longer what Kant believed to be "absolutely" unknowable, but what men _discover_ to be what is merely unknowable _in itself_ through its endlessly _partial revelation_. Yet this very manifestation of the part _alone_ and _not_ of the whole of being--this revealed _lack of unity_ of being in the presence of human consciousness--is what constitutes and discloses its _nonrationality_ to that consciousness. Kant's phenomenon had only hidden this nonrationality; that of his Existential heirs and their successors now at last unveils it: "La différence," Camus himself states in Le Mythe de Sisyphe, "c'est qu'il n'y a pas de scénario, mais _une illustration successive et inconséquente_" (MS: 130).⁴⁴ Thus in the post-Kantian era, rational man uncovers that _incoherence of reality_ which in his unrelenting will to order he had _concealed_ from himself by _creating_ that order; and he comes to realize as a result that both this will and its creation were the unconscious expression of his instinctive and all-con-

suming desire for meaning in an all but meaningless and
hence intolerable world:

> . . . l'esprit qui cherche à comprendre la
> réalité ne peut s'estimer satisfait que s'il
> la réduit en termes de pensée. . . .
> Penser, c'est avant tout vouloir créer un
> monde (ou limiter le sien, ce qui revient au
> même). C'est partir du désaccord fondamental
> qui sépare l'homme de son expérience pour
> trouver un terrain d'entente selon sa nostal-
> gie, un univers corseté de raisons ou éclairé
> d'analogies qui permette de résoudre le di-
> vorce insupportable. Le philosophe, même
> s'il est Kant, est créateur. (MS: 110,
> 177)[45]

And yet accordingly, says Camus, this is man in retreat
from himself as well as from the world, for he is increasingly aware of the fact that his own revelation of
being substantially conceals it from him, thus disclos-
ing that it is he, as much as the world of which he is
conscious, who constitutes the gulf between himself and
that world.[46] And so his immediate impulse is to transcend his own rationality by so sharpening and extend-
ing its outline of the being which he perceives as to
conceal the disconnectedness of that being, or nearly
every trace of the being itself. This is a "cover-up"
by the critical philosophy which Camus then proceeds to
vigorously expose in the critical spirit of that philosophy, setting against Kant's tragic idealism the
tragic realism which it clearly anticipates:

> Il faut considérer comme une perpétuelle ré-

> férence . . . le décalage constant entre ce
> que nous imaginons savoir et ce que nous sa-
> vons réellement, le consentement pratique et
> l'ignorance simulée qui fait que nous vivons
> avec des idées qui, si nous les éprouvions
> vraiment, devraient bouleverser toute notre
> vie. . . . Tant que l'esprit se tait dans le
> monde immobile de ses espoirs, tout se re-
> flète et s'ordonne dans l'unité de sa nostal-
> gie. Mais à son premier mouvement, ce monde
> se fêle et s'écroule: une infinité d'éclats
> miroitants s'offrent à la connaissance. . . .
> . . . ces catégories qui expliquent tout
> . . . n'ont rien à voir avec l'esprit.
> [Elles] nient sa vérité profonde qui est
> d'être enchaîné. . . . L'absurde dépend au-
> tant de l'homme que du monde. Il est pour le
> moment leur seul lien. Il les scelle l'un à
> l'autre comme la haine seule peut river les
> êtres. (MS: 110-111, 113)⁴⁷

Jean-Paul Sartre, the dean of contemporary Existentialism in France, is to say no more than this when in L'Etre et le Néant he avows that the "pure, nihilated conditions" in which human consciousness delimits and reveals the phenomenon of being are themselves the barrier between that consciousness and the total being of the phenomenon:

> "Il y a" de l'être parce que je suis négation
> de l'être et la mondanité, la spatialité, la
> quantité, l'ustensilité, la temporalité ne
> viennent à l'être que parce que je suis néga-
> tion de l'être, elles n'ajoutent rien à
> l'être, elles sont de pures conditions néan-
> tisées du "il y a", elles ne font que réali-
> ser le il y a. Mais ces conditions qui ne
> sont rien me séparent plus radicalement de
> l'être que ne le feraient des déformations
> prismatiques à travers lesquelles je pourrais
> encore espérer le découvrir. Dire qu'il y a
> de l'être n'est rien et pourtant c'est opérer
> une totale métamorphose, puisqu'il n'y a
> d'être que pour un Pour-soi. Ce n'est pas

> dans sa qualité propre que l'être est <u>relatif</u>
> au Pour-soi, ni dans son être, et par <u>là nous</u>
> échappons au relativisme kantien; mais c'est
> dans son "il y a", puisque dans sa négation
> interne, le Pour-soi affirme ce qui ne peut
> s'affirmer, connaît l'être <u>tel</u> <u>qu'il est</u>
> alors que le "tel qu'il est" ne saurait ap-
> partenir à l'être. En ce sens, à la fois le
> Pour-soi est présence immédiate à l'être et,
> à la fois, il se glisse comme une distance
> infinie entre lui-même et l'être. C'est que
> le connaître a pour idéal l'être-ce-qu'on-
> connaît et pour structure originelle le ne-
> pas-être-ce-qui-est-connu. Mondanité, spa-
> tialité, etc., ne font qu'exprimer ce ne-pas-
> être. Ainsi je me retrouve partout entre moi
> et l'être comme le rien qui <u>n'est</u> <u>pas</u> l'être.
> (<u>EN</u>: 269-270)[48]

Thus quite like the Existentialists and in clear contradistinction to Kant, Camus fully recognizes that rational man is alienated both from the <u>world</u> which he reveals and from <u>himself</u> as precisely he who reveals it: "Etranger à moi-même et à ce monde, [je suis] armé pour tout secours d'une pensée qui se nie elle-même dès qu'elle affirme" (<u>MS</u>: 112).[49] And yet he then somewhat rhetorically poses the following question as to the ul- timate <u>raison</u> <u>d'être</u> of this twofold alienation: "Quelle <u>est</u> cette condition," he asks, "où je ne puis avoir la paix qu'en refusant de savoir et de vivre, où l'appétit de conquête se heurte à des murs qui défient ses assauts" (<u>MS</u>: 112)?[50] As he well knew, it is the "human condition," the condition, that is, of man with- out God, for the world's nonrationality is the <u>absence</u> of God, the absence from the world of he whom Apostolos

Makrakis called "the Logos and analogy (or the Reason and proportion)."[51] He is the Word, according to John, through whom "all things were made"[52] and thus filled with meaning. "Privé de la volonté divine," Camus himself later observed in L'Homme Révolté, "le monde est privé également d'unité et de finalité" (HR: 476).[53] But as he showed elsewhere in the same work, it was not that contemporary philosophy to which his own ideas were so intimately related that first discovered this absence, but the thought of the European Enlightenment from which they both derived: "[C'est] à partir du moment où le christianisme, au sortir de sa période triomphante, s'est trouvé soumis à la critique de la raison, dans la mesure exacte où la divinité du Christ a été niée, [que] la douleur est redevenue le lot des hommes" (HR: 446). Thus the modern notion of the senselessness of man's suffering and hence of the absurdity of his existence is rooted in what Hegel termed "the negative procedure of the Enlightenment"[54]--in the critical denial, that is, of one of the central tenets of patristic philosophy enunciated in Paul's Epistle to the Romans: that of the inherent rationality and hence of the divine origin of being. Therewith, "the invisible things of him from the creation of the world" are no longer "clearly seen," for they are not "understood by the things that are made," not "even his eternal power and Godhead."55

Consequently, if by way of criticism the contingency or the utter fortuitousness of the <u>world</u> was revealed, it could not but follow that the being who revealed it should then reveal <u>himself</u> to be contingent as well: "Je connais une autre évidence," says Camus in <u>Le Mythe</u>: "elle me dit que l'homme est mortel. . . . [Et] sous l'éclairage mortel de cette destinée, l'inutilité apparaît" (<u>MS</u>: 110, 109). And yet those very categories of the subject with which criticism had replaced the objective world-order of the Church Fathers are then <u>themselves</u> disclosed to be quite useless and irrelevant before the inexorable and all-important fact of man's mortality in the absence of God:

> Juger que la vie vaut ou ne vaut pas la peine d'être vécue, c'est répondre à la question fondamentale de la philosophie. Le reste, si le monde a trois dimensions, si l'esprit a neuf ou douze catégories, vient ensuite. Ce sont des jeux. . . .
> . . . aucun effort n'[est] <u>a priori</u> justifiable devant les sanglantes mathématiques qui ordonnent notre condition. (<u>MS</u>: 99, 109)56

Thus, it may well be said of Camus what he then himself sympathetically observes of his Existential contemporary, Martin Heidegger:

> Il s'intéresse à Kant, mais c'est pour reconnaître le caractère borné de sa "Raison pure". C'est pour conclure au terme de ses analyses que "le monde ne peut plus rien of-

> frir à l'homme angoissé". Ce souci lui paraît à tel point dépasser en vérité les catégories du raisonnement qu'il ne songe qu'à lui et ne parle que de lui. . . . Lui non plus ne sépare pas la conscience de l'absurde. (MS: 115)[57]

And yet as we have seen, man's realization that he is himself a part of the absurd that he seeks to dispel has often led him to what Camus--here so unlike his age and as a true descendant of the lumières--holds to be that for which even his predecessors were not entirely blameless: namely, to the irrational attempt to dissociate oneself from the evidence.[58] But the mood of modern man is no longer one of mere disquietude allayed by the consolations of what was all too readily deemed to be an efficacious, if confessedly limited reason[59]; rather, it is one of angry frustration at what is at last disclosed to be this reason's utter powerlessness to resolve that fundamental enigma of his condition so well expressed by the character Caligula in Camus's play of the same name. "C'est une vérité toute simple et toute claire, un peu bête, mais difficile à découvrir et lourde à porter," he declares. "Les hommes meurent et ils ne sont pas heureux" (CAL: 16). But in his violent desperation for meaning Caligula "logically" rejects the very lucidity that reveals this truth by fleeing from a world the contingency of whose being is a constant reminder of both his own and that of all men:

> Il est vrai. Mais je ne le savais pas auparavant. Maintenant, je sais. . . . Ce monde, tel qu'il est fait, n'est pas supportable. J'ai donc besoin de la lune, ou du bonheur, ou de l'immortalité, de quelque chose qui soit dément peut-être, mais qui ne soit pas de ce monde. . . .
> Les hommes pleurent parce que les choses ne sont pas ce qu'elles devraient être.
> (CAL: 15, 26)[60]

Yet the very identification of his own condition with that of all humanity so revolts him <u>against</u> his fellow men that his "flight" from what he painfully knows to be an inescapable world consists in the vengeful and nihilistic will to "transform" it by destroying them and those intrinsically-human values which prove that <u>they alone</u> are the source of whatever meaning they may perceive in it. Thus, to the eternal subjectivity of such meaning as <u>evidence</u> of the absurd Caligula far prefers its total <u>dissolution</u> in the murder of its "culpable" authors; and he claims total justification for his act in the total absence of transcendent values <u>implied</u> by this subjectivity[61]:

> [Vous] donne[z] de l'importance aux êtres et aux choses. Voilà ce que je ne puis vous pardonner. . . .
> Ce monde est sans importance et qui le reconnaît conquiert sa liberté. . . . Et justement, je vous hais parce que vous n'êtes pas libres. . . .
> Il suffit que je remue la langue pour que tout redevienne noir et que les êtres me répugnent. . . .

> Je veux mêler le ciel à la mer, confondre laideur et beauté, faire jaillir le rire de la souffrance. . . .
> Ma volonté est de . . . changer [le monde]. Je ferai à ce siècle le don de l'égalité. Et lorsque tout sera aplani, l'impossible enfin sur terre, la lune dans mes mains, alors, peut-être, moi-même je serai transformé et le monde avec moi. . . .
> (CAL: 25, 26, 27)62

For Caligula, then, murder and the desolation of all that is presently human--acts logically permitted in what is an objectively senseless world--are themselves the means to its final <u>disintegration</u> as such and to its <u>recreation</u> as the <u>antithesis</u> of itself. In an order bereft of God, he requires the elimination of all that is finite in man, so that man may <u>become</u> God, that he may then fill it with meaning. But in this world <u>without</u> meaning <u>Caligula</u> becomes God, and as the supreme judge of all initiates a reign of terror against those who now inhabit it in the name of their posterity:

> Et que me fait une main ferme, de quoi me sert ce pouvoir si étonnant si je ne puis changer l'ordre des choses, si je ne puis faire que le soleil se couche à l'est, que la souffrance décroisse et que les êtres ne meurent plus? Non, . . . il est indifférent de dormir ou de rester éveillé, si je n'ai pas d'action sur l'ordre de ce monde. . . .
> Et . . . qu'est-ce qu'un dieu pour que je désire m'<u>égaler</u> à lui? Ce que je désire de toutes mes forces, aujourd'hui, est <u>au-dessus</u> des dieux. Je prends en charge un royaume où l'impossible est roi. . . .
> . . . alors enfin les hommes ne mourront pas et ils seront heureux. . . .

> Faites entrer les coupables. Il me faut
> des coupables. Et ils le sont tous. (CAL:
> 27, 28)⁶³

This attitude clearly reflects the view of the Grand Inquisitors described by Camus in L'Homme Révolté. "Le royaume des cieux viendra, en effet, sur terre," he writes, "mais les hommes y régneront, quelques-uns d'abord qui seront les Césars, ceux qui ont compris les premiers, et tous les autres ensuite, avec le temps. L'unité de la création se fera, par tous les moyens, puisque tout est permis" (HR: 470). The Inquisitors are the self-appointed Caesars of our time, the regents of a yet imperfect race who teach it that humanity is itself the means to its own divinity through the elimination of those elements within it that resist its will to power. "Dieu mort, il faut changer et organiser le monde par les forces de l'homme. La seule force de l'imprécation n'y suffisant plus, il faut des armes et la conquête de la totalité" (HR: 517). Thus for the forces of purity in a world that is still impure, impurity is the only means to its purification. "Rien n'est pur, ce cri convulse le siècle," observes Camus. "L'impur, donc l'histoire, va devenir la règle et la terre déserte sera livrée à la force toute nue qui décidera ou non de la divinité de l'homme" (HR: 543).⁶⁴ In a world that is still without values because there is no God, history is the only rule, the rule of power to become God. If God is yet to be, then so are his values; history is their unbridled becoming, a becoming whose end is their realization. And so as the means to its own end, it is justified by this end: it is the crime to end all crime. "L'humanité, à travers les crimes, les violences et la mort, marche vers cette consommation qui justifiera tout" (HR: 596-597). But if the end for which humanity commits these crimes against itself is self-perfection, then these crimes are its act of atonement for being imperfect: they are the means through which humanity purges itself of those forces within it that persist in the sin of being all too human in an all but meaningless world. For so long as the individual continues to be what he is, then so does the race of which he is a part. And so at the same time that the individual suffers for his recalcitrance at the hands of the race, the race suffers at the hands of the individual in its effort to subdue him. Thus until the unity of mankind is achieved, all men are guilty, and must pay for their guilt in order to achieve it. History is the expiation of their guilt; its consummation is the achievement of their unity. If God does not exist, then history is the way to salvation; but if all men are guilty, then the way is long and hard. "'L'affaire n'est qu'au début,'" says the Inquisitor, "'elle est loin d'être terminée,

et la terre aura encore beaucoup à souffrir, mais nous
atteindrons notre but, nous serons César, alors nous
songerons au bonheur universel'" (HR: 470).65 If all
of mankind is guilty and there is no God to save it,
then it must so atone for its guilt as to become God,
and save itself. For the sin of being in a world without God is that of not being God, of being no more than
what one is without God: redemption from the sin of
being oneself is self-transcendence. But then in order
to transcend himself, each individual requires the support of every other. The salvation of men is their
unity: self-transcendence is the deification of the
race. "Il s'agit de déifier l'espèce comme Nietzsche
et de prendre en charge son idéal de surhumanité afin
d'assurer le salut de tous" (HR: 517). The task is
herculean, for it requires no less than the sacrifice
of what men value the most, and of what has been the
source of perpetual conflict among them: their individuality. They will meet the crusade with fierce resistance, and it will suffer countless setbacks in its
effort to convert them. But it will gradually gain in
momentum, for not even man's concern for personal freedom can repress his desire for divinity. "Mais rien,"
remarks Camus, "ne peut décourager l'appétit de divinité au coeur de l'homme" (HR: 555).66 The number of
crusaders will increase, and they will be as one, but

at the price that each must pay for the sin of self-interest: himself. Until the unity of all of mankind is achieved, they must suffer the punishment of serving as the means to its achievement by punishing and converting the many who still oppose them. The sacrifice of others entails the sacrifice of oneself as well. "La soif d'unité doit se réaliser, même dans la fosse commune," says Camus. "S'ils tuent des hommes, c'est qu'ils refusent la condition mortelle et veulent l'immortalité pour tous. Ils se tuent alors d'une certaine manière" (HR: 649). The history of men, therefore, is their mutual punishment for what they are until they become what they will be. "A sa manière, l'histoire n'est qu'un long châtiment puisque la vraie récompense ne sera savourée qu'à la fin des temps" (HR: 644). Until all men are divine, no man is of any value in himself, but only as a tool of history, as a part of that process through which he and all others serve to purify the race by their common suffering and death, that it may then become divine. The negation by individuals of each other dissolves them in the race until the race consumes itself in its own blood, that it may thereby cleanse and transform itself. It is the role of all men, therefore, to devour and assimilate each other until they see in each other the reflection of the God that they will all have become. "L'*homo homini lupus*," says Camus summing up the thought of Feuerbach, "devient alors homo homini deus" (HR: 553). If the sin of humanity in a world without God is no less than that of being human and of not being God, then it is only by dehumanizing itself that humanity can atone for its sin, and become God. Thus, only through the degradation by each of every other can the dignity of all be achieved. "Telle est la mission du prolétariat: faire surgir la suprême dignité de la suprême humiliation," writes Camus with reference to the thought of Karl Marx. "Par ses douleurs et ses luttes, il est le Christ humain qui rachète le péché collectif de l'aliénation. Il est, d'abord, le porteur innombrable de la négation totale, le héraut de l'affirmation définitive ensuite" (HR: 610).[67] If it is true that men are as nothing compared to the idea of what they will be but that their very nothingness constitutes an almost insurmountable gulf between themselves and the idea, then no sacrifice of their lives is too high a price to pay for its realization. "Qu'importe en effet le sacrifice des hommes s'il doit servir au salut de l'humanité entière" (HR: 609)! The terrorist Stepan echoes this thought in Les Justes: "Qu'importe si nous . . . aimons assez fort [la révolution] pour l'imposer à l'humanité entière et la sauver d'elle-même et de son esclavage" (J: 336).[68] All of humanity, therefore, is itself the sacrifice it must make in order to save itself; indeed, nothing less than its death is required for its resurrection. Camus aptly summarizes this view in the <u>Actuelles</u>: "Tuons tout le monde," he writes, "au nom de la justice pour tous" (<u>AII</u>: 720).69 All men must be absorbed by the very process of the history which they make in order that it may transform them, that they may thereby transform the nature of which they are a part. "L'histoire, précisément, se distingue de la nature en ce qu'elle la transforme par les moyens de la volonté, de la science et de la passion. . . . Déjà, par le travail, par la transformation du monde naturel en monde technique, [l'homme] s'affranchit de cette nature qui était au principe de son esclavage puisqu'il n'avait pas su s'élever au-dessus d'elle par l'acceptation de la mort" (<u>HR</u>: 603, 548). Thus history as the source of unity among men becomes the source of unity between men and nature as well. "Le règne de l'histoire commence," says Camus, "et, s'identifiant à sa seule histoire, l'homme . . . se vouera désormais aux révolutions nihilistes du XXe siècle qui, niant toute morale, cherchent désespérément l'unité du genre humain à travers une épuisante accumulation de crimes et de guerres. . . . les révolutions cyniques, qu'elles soient de droite ou de gauche, . . . vont tenter de conquérir l'unité du monde pour fonder enfin la religion de l'homme. Tout ce qui était à Dieu sera désormais rendu à César" (HR: 540). In a world without God, each individual must submit every other to the will of history so that all may submit to their own will the nature of which they are a part, that all may then become God in his place. "Puisque le salut de l'homme ne se fait pas en Dieu, il doit se faire sur la terre. Puisque le monde n'a pas de direction, l'homme, à partir du moment où il l'accepte, doit lui en donner une, qui aboutisse à une humanité supérieure" (HR: 487). In order, then, that all may become supermen, each must make a sub-man of every other, "'une totale soumission et une totale immolation de lui-même à la voracité sacrée du devenir'" (CII: 298).[70] "Pour que l'homme devienne dieu," remarks Camus, "il faut que la victime s'abaisse à devenir bourreau" (HR: 581). Thus consumed by the very process of history through which it seeks to transcend itself, all of mankind is stripped of its humanity. "Le grand drame de l'homme d'Occident," writes Camus in the Actuelles, "c'est qu'entre lui et son devenir historique, ne s'interposent plus ni les forces de la nature ni celles de l'amitié. Ses racines coupées, ses bras desséchés, il se confond déjà avec les potences qui lui sont promises" (AI: 403).[71] The very means of history, then, become the end for which it works[72]: history as the crime to end all crime is crime itself. "La logique de l'histoire, à partir du moment où elle est acceptée totalement," affirms Camus, "la mène, peu à peu, . . . à mutiler l'homme de plus en plus, et à se transformer elle-même en crime objectif" (HR: 648).73 But then a total acceptance of history implies a total rejection of man, for if history is the way to men's salvation and the salvation of men is their unity, then history is the negation of all that defines them as human: their individuality. Each, then, must cease to be what he is in order that all may become what they will be. "Notre révolution," says Camus, "est une tentative pour conquérir un être neuf, par le faire, hors de toute règle morale. C'est pourquoi elle se condamne à ne vivre que pour l'histoire, et dans la terreur. L'homme n'est rien, selon elle, s'il n'obtient pas dans l'histoire, de gré ou de force, le consentement unanime" (HR: 652).74 And so the longer men continue to be what they are, the more must all be reduced to what they are not; so that if all men do not become what they must be, then all must die. If man cannot cease to be what he is, then he must cease to be: if he can be no more than what he is in a world without God, then he is deserving of death. This, Camus tells us, is the logic of nihilism. "Jeté contre les limites du monde," he writes, "le [nihiliste] choisit d'abord l'apocalypse et la destruction, plutôt que d'accepter la règle impossible qui le fait ce qu'il est dans le monde tel qu'il va. . . . Ne pouvant réparer l'injustice par l'édification de la justice, [il] préfère au moins la noyer dans une injustice encore plus générale qui se confond enfin avec l'anéantissement. . . . A ce degré d'indignation, la raison devient fureur" (HR: 491, 492, 509-510). This, too, therefore, is the logic of historicism. "La pensée qui se forme avec la seule histoire . . . enlèv[e] à l'homme . . . la raison de vivre. [Elle] le pousse à l'extrême déchéance du 'pourquoi vivre'" (HR: 651).[75] Far worse, indeed, than the limited reason it sought to replace, historical reason is irrational. "La raison historique," says Camus, "est une raison irrationnelle et romantique" (HR: 625).[76] "Votre raison ou les charniers," he retorts against the Marxist Emmanuel d'Astier de la Vigerie, "voilà l'avenir que vous tracez" (AI: 367).[77]

Against Hegel and Feuerbach, Marx, Nietzsche, and Spengler, the first, third, and fourth of whom he calls "les mauvais génies de l'Europe d'aujourd'hui" (ESS: 1341),[78] Camus argues that if man can be no more than what he is in a world without meaning, it is because this world can be no more than what he is not, for **he alone** is meaningful in wishing to give it a meaning, and this meaning is himself. "Vous n'avez jamais cru au sens de ce monde et vous en avez tiré l'idée que tout était équivalent et que le bien et le mal se définissaient selon qu'on le voulait," he writes in the last of his <u>Lettres</u> <u>à</u> <u>un</u> <u>ami</u> <u>allemand</u>. "Je <u>continue</u> à croire que ce monde n'a pas de sens supérieur. Mais je sais que quelque chose en lui a du sens et c'est l'homme, parce qu'il est le seul être à exiger d'en avoir" (<u>LAA</u>: 240, 241).[79] And so if only man has a meaning as the only part of the world in pursuit of its meaning, then only he can be the source of the meaning he pursues; so that the world may not be meaningful, but man is that part of the world that <u>makes</u> it meaningful. "Ce monde a du moins la vérité de l'homme," says Camus, "et notre tâche est de lui donner ses raisons contre le destin lui-même" (<u>LAA</u>: 241). The world can be meaningful, therefore, <u>only</u> insofar as man is a part of it. "Et il n'a pas <u>d'autres</u> raisons que <u>l'homme</u> et c'est celui-ci qu'il faut sauver si l'on veut sauver l'idée qu'on se fait de la vie" (<u>LAA</u>: 241).[80] Hence he is not to be saved from, but <u>for</u> himself. "Qu'est-ce sauver l'homme? . . . c'est ne pas le mutiler et c'est donner ses chances à la justice qu'il est le seul à concevoir" (<u>LAA</u>: 241). In a world without that justice of which only man can conceive, the only end of man is man himself; so that history is not the "becoming," but man is the <u>being</u> of all values.[81]

"[Les hommes] savent justement," says Camus in L'Eté, "qu'il n'est pas de justice aveugle, que l'histoire est sans yeux et qu'il faut donc rejeter sa justice pour lui substituer, autant qu'il se peut, celle que l'esprit conçoit" (ETE: 843).[82] True justice is never "blind," for it can only be conceived by a rational being in the face of what is not rational, by man, for example, in the face of the history that denies him. "L'histoire, dans son mouvement pur, ne fournit par elle-même aucune valeur. . . . Le révolté, loin de faire un absolu de l'histoire, la récuse et la met en contestation, au nom d'une idée qu'il a de sa propre nature" (HR: 692, 693). This idea of his own nature for which man rebels against history is that he is rational, and rational because he is human, so that he cannot but dispute that which pretends to save men by killing them. "Rational nature," says Kant, "is distinguished from the rest of nature by this, that it sets before itself an end."[83] In a nonrational world, rational man is not a mere means to the end for which he works, but the end itself, and so one for which he cannot work but by humanizing this world. As Camus writes in his essay on revolt, "l'homme révolté est . . . appliqué à revendiquer un ordre humain où toutes les réponses soient humaines, c'est-à-dire raisonnablement formulées" (HR: 430).[84] The answers in a genuinely <u>human</u> order, therefore, cannot be reasonable for one man without being reasonable for all other men as well; so that if one man is an end in himself, every and all other men are ends in themselves, whence the categorical imperative of Kant in his <u>Fundamental Principles of the Metaphysic of Morals</u>: "The foundation of this principle is: <u>rational nature exists as an end in itself</u>. Man necessarily conceives his own existence as being so. . . . But every other rational being regards its existence similarly, just on the same rational principle that holds for me. . . . Accordingly the practical imperative will be as follows: <u>So act as to treat humanity, whether in thine own person or in that of any other, in every case as an end withal, never as means only</u>."[85] Camus echoes this thought in <u>L'Homme Révolté</u>: "Comment, sans une concession remarquable au goût du confort," he asks, "conserver pour soi le bénéfice <u>exclusif</u> d'un tel raisonnement? Dès l'instant où ce bien est reconnu comme tel, il est celui de tous les hommes. . . . L'individu n'est donc pas, à lui seul, cette valeur qu'il veut défendre. Il faut, au moins, tous les hommes pour la composer. Dans la révolte, l'homme se dépasse en autrui et, de ce point de vue, la solidarité humaine est métaphysique" (<u>HR</u>: 416, 426).[86] Here, indeed, Camus more specifically alludes to the "<u>raisonnement</u>" of <u>Le Mythe de Sisyphe</u>: "Pour dire que la vie est absurde, la conscience a besoin d'être vivante" (<u>HR</u>: 416)--and the "<u>bien</u>" to which he refers--"le seul bien nécessaire" (<u>HR</u>: 416)--is life itself, for while it <u>is</u> absurd, life is also that without which there would be no consciousness <u>perceiving</u> it to be so, and thereby distinguishing itself and all others from the rest of the world as <u>ends in themselves</u>. "Car tout commence par la conscience," says Camus in <u>Le Mythe</u>, "et rien ne vaut que par elle" (<u>MS</u>: 107); so that "life" may not be meaningful, but in living man himself is that part of his life that <u>makes</u> it meaningful.87 And this is what Kant means when he states that if "there were something <u>whose existence</u> has <u>in itself</u> an absolute worth, something which, being <u>an end in itself</u>, could be a source of definite laws, then in this and this alone would lie the source of a possible categorical imperative. . . . Now I say: man . . . <u>exists</u> as an end in himself."88

And this is to say, in turn, that he is himself the end for which he exists and not the mere means to that end, that he is the means to the end <u>as the end itself</u>, hence <u>the end itself</u> as means, his own end as his own means.89 As the mere means of one another, both one and the other become the means to an end <u>other</u> than themselves and the humanity of which they are a part; they serve an end that cannot but be irrational in a world whose only <u>rational</u> end is man himself. As Camus writes of man in <u>Le Mythe</u>, "un peuple d'irrationnels s'est dressé et l'entoure jusqu'à sa fin dernière. . . . Le monde est <u>peuplé</u> de ces irrationnels. A lui seul dont je ne comprends pas la signification unique, il n'est qu'un immense irrationnel. . . . Mais . . . l'homme garde . . . sa <u>clairvoyance</u> et la connaissance précise des murs qui l'entourent. . . . Cette discipline que l'esprit se dicte à lui-même, cette volonté forgée de toutes pièces, ce face-à-face, ont quelque chose de puissant et de <u>singulier</u>. . . . Oui, l'homme est sa <u>propre</u> fin. Et il est sa <u>seule</u> fin. . . . Cette heure qui est comme une respiration et qui revient aussi sûrement que son malheur, cette heure est celle de la <u>conscience</u>. A chacun de ces instants, . . . il est <u>supérieur</u> à son destin. Il est plus <u>fort</u> que son rocher" (<u>MS</u>: 113, 117, 139, 166, 196).[90] The dignity of man, therefore, consists in his rationality, or in being <u>precisely</u> <u>what</u> <u>he</u> <u>is</u> and what the world is not; and here Camus again echoes Kant, who states that "whatever has a value can be replaced by something else which is <u>equivalent</u>. . . . but that which constitutes the condition under which alone anything can be an end in itself, this has not merely a relative worth, i.e. value, but an intrinsic worth, that is <u>dignity</u>. . . . Thus . . . humanity . . . is that which alone has dig-

nity. . . . nature . . . contains [nothing] which . . .
it could put in [the] place [of humanity], for [the
latter's] worth consists . . . in the disposition of
mind, that is, the maxims of the will."91 In this,
however, not only does Camus echo Kant, but both Kant
and Camus echo Pascal:

> L'homme n'est qu'un roseau, le plus faible de
> la nature; mais c'est un roseau pensant. Il
> ne faut pas que l'univers entier s'arme pour
> l'écraser: une vapeur, une goutte d'eau,
> suffit pour le tuer. Mais, quand l'univers
> l'écraserait, l'homme serait encore plus
> noble que ce qui le tue, parce qu'il sait
> qu'il meurt, et l'avantage que l'univers a
> sur lui; l'univers n'en sait rien.
> Toute notre dignité consiste donc en la
> pensée. . . . Travaillons donc à bien pen-
> ser: voilà le principe de la morale.92

But already in Le Mythe, and in contradistinction to
both Pascal and the Existentialists who followed him,
Camus returns to the idea of a properly human nature
that the very dignity of man implies--an idea deriving
from the Greeks and reappearing in both Kant and the
French lumières.93 "La seule dignité de l'homme," he
writes, "[c'est] la révolte tenace contre sa condition"
(MS: 190-191),94 thereby affirming that while rational
man is "unsettled" in his being by the nonrational
world that confronts him, it is no less the rationality
of man--his own rational nature--that sets him apart
from it. "Et qu'est-ce qui fait le fond de ce conflit,
de cette fracture entre le monde et mon esprit," asks

Camus, "sinon la conscience que j'en ai" (MS: 136)?[95]
Man, therefore, is his own justification against the
world; and this is aptly expressed by Camus with the
following quotation from Euripides in the Carnets:
"'Voici le moment de prouver par des actes que la dignité de l'homme ne le cède pas à la grandeur des
dieux.' (Iphigénie en Tauride.)" (CI: 235).[96] The justification of men, that is, consists in the justification by each of every other man as an end in himself;
so that if I rebel, then I do so for all of mankind.
"Je me révolte," says Camus, "donc nous sommes" (HR:
432). I rebel for what, in the phrase of Kant, is my
own "intrinsic worth" and that of the humanity of which
I am a part, for that to which Camus refers as "quelque
chose en [moi] . . . qui ne [m']appartient pas seulement, mais qui est un lieu commun où tous les hommes
. . . ont une communauté prête" (HR: 425-426). This
intrinsic worth as the common ground of the race of men
is the very nature of the race itself: its human nature. As Camus states in L'Homme Révolté, "une prise
de conscience naît du mouvement de révolte: la perception, soudain éclatante, qu'il y a dans l'homme quelque
chose à quoi l'homme peut s'identifier. . . . L'analyse de la révolte conduit au moins au soupçon qu'il y
a une nature humaine, comme le pensaient les Grecs, et
contrairement aux postulats de la pensée contemporaine.

Pourquoi se révolter s'il n'y a, en soi, rien de permanent à préserver" (HR: 424, 425)?⁹⁷ It follows, then, that the only sin of being in a world without God is that, not of not being God, but of not being what one is without God.⁹⁸ "Mais comment éviter de tourmenter les hommes," argues Camus, "si l'on a décidé d'en faire des dieux? . . . au lieu de tuer et mourir pour produire l'être que nous ne sommes pas, nous avons à vivre et faire vivre pour créer ce que nous sommes" (HR: 582, 653).⁹⁹ Man, therefore, is not guilty of what he is or of what the world is not, but innocent of being in a world that is not what he is. "On voudrait lui faire reconnaître sa culpabilité," writes Camus in Le Mythe. "Lui se sent innocent. A vrai dire, il ne sent que cela, son innocence irréparable" (MS: 137).¹⁰⁰ Indeed, his innocence is as irreparable as his nature is permanent. "Le vieux avait raison, les hommes étaient toujours les mêmes," affirms the narrator at the end of La Peste. "Mais c'était leur force et leur innocence et c'est ici que, par-dessus toute douleur, Rieux sentait qu'il les rejoignait. . . . le docteur Rieux décida alors de rédiger le récit qui s'achève ici, . . . pour dire simplement ce qu'on apprend au milieu des fléaux, qu'il y a dans les hommes plus de choses à admirer que de choses à mépriser" (P: 1473).¹⁰¹ And as it follows that there are more things to admire in man than all the "plagues" of the world that beset him, they are the only things in this world that are worthy of admiration; and there is no admiration of which they are worthy but that for one another of those who possess them, so that in possessing them they possess each other as their only value; and from this value is born their solidarity in defense of man against a world that denies him. "Le fondement de cette valeur est la révolte elle-même," reasons Camus. "La solidarité des hommes se fonde sur le mouvement de révolte et celui-ci, à son tour, ne trouve de justification que dans cette complicité. . . . Le premier progrès d'un esprit saisi d'étrangeté est donc de reconnaître qu'il partage cette étrangeté avec tous les hommes et que la réalité humaine, dans sa totalité, souffre de cette distance par rapport à soi et au monde. Le mal qui éprouvait un seul homme devient peste collective. Dans l'épreuve quotidienne qui est la nôtre, la révolte joue le même rôle que le 'cogito' dans l'ordre de la pensée: elle est la première évidence. Mais cette évidence tire l'individu de sa solitude. Elle est un lieu commun qui fonde sur tous les hommes la première valeur" (HR: 431, 432).[102]

And so as we saw in the first part of this essay, ethics is of prime importance in the thought of Camus, as it was in that of both the Greeks and their philosophical descendants of the eighteenth century.[103] Yet for the Greeks as well as for the philosophes the realm of epistemology was more nearly as important as that of ethics, for in the minds of both the two were inevitably linked. As the historian Peter Gay rightly points out, the Greeks "had looked in two directions--outward: to nature, objective universal law--in a word, to science; and inward: to self-knowledge, inner clarity--in a word, to morality"; while the philosophes, in turn, had "regarded the scientific revolution of their own age as more than a game or merely abstract knowledge-- as is evident from their rather confused moral demands on science, they hoped it would become the prelude, and even the servant, of moral and political improvement."[104] And this was the hope, as we have seen, of Immanuel Kant.[105] But it could no longer be that of Camus, for by his time the protective limits of the critical philosophy had become the object of its own criticism, thus transforming the subjective idealism of Kant into the idealistic subjectivism of those ideologies to which he was so long opposed.[106] But to these ideologies, for which all men submit the world to their own will by submitting each other to the will of history, Camus opposes that tragically realistic view of the world which they reject, but which the critical philossophy, despite its own "cover-up," had itself anticipated as the only rational alternative to them: the acceptance, that is, of the world's <u>irremediable</u> absurdity.[107] But it is this acceptance, or what we have called the tragic realism of Camus, that makes the rationalism of his predecessors even <u>more</u> pragmatic than it was, transforming it into an ethical pragmatism. "La plus grande économie qu'on puisse réaliser dans l'ordre de la pensée," writes Camus in the <u>Carnets</u>, "c'est d'accepter la non-intelligibilité du monde--et de s'occuper de l'homme" (<u>CII</u>: 113).[108] "A l'aube des temps modernes: Tout est consommé?" he asks. "D'accord, alors commençons de vivre" (<u>CI</u>: 205).

And this is to say that if we <u>are</u> to live, then we can only do so <u>in</u> the world, however unintelligible it may be. "Et pourtant," says Cherea to Caligula, "il faut bien <u>plaider</u> pour ce monde, si nous <u>voulons</u> y vivre" (<u>CAL</u>: 25).[109] To argue in favor of the world, then, is to do so in favor of man as its only end; and to work for that end is to do no more than <u>humanize</u> the world, since any attempt to "transform" it can only result in the <u>negation</u> of the end itself. "La logique du révolté," affirms Camus, "est de vouloir servir la justice pour ne pas ajouter à l'injustice de la condition, de s'efforcer au langage clair pour ne pas épaissir le mensonge universel et de parier, face à la douleur des hommes, pour le bonheur. La passion nihiliste, ajoutant à l'injustice et au mensonge, détruit dans sa rage son exigence ancienne et s'enlève ainsi les raisons les plus claires de sa révolte. Elle tue, folle de sentir que ce monde est livré à la mort" (HR: 688-689). But then for an angrily frustrated nihilism the very negation of man as end becomes the end itself, its own logic dictating that if man is mortal, then it is he who is <u>responsible</u> for his mortality, and so <u>deserving</u> of it. "Il y a apparemment les révoltés qui veulent mourir et ceux qui veulent faire mourir," remarks Camus. "Mais ce sont les mêmes, brûlés du désir de la vraie vie, frustrés de l'être et préférant alors l'injustice généralisée à une justice mutilée" (HR: 509), a justice "mutilated," that is, by man himself.[110] And it is for this the "final solution" of the German ideologues that Camus impassionedly indicts them in the <u>name</u> of man at the end of his <u>Lettres</u> <u>à</u> <u>un</u> <u>ami</u> <u>allemand</u>:

> . . . vous admettiez assez l'injustice de notre condition pour vous résoudre à y ajouter, tandis qu'il m'apparaissait au contraire que l'homme devait affirmer la justice pour lutter contre l'injustice éternelle, créer du bonheur pour protester contre l'univers du malheur. Parce que vous avez fait de votre désespoir une ivresse, parce que vous vous en êtes délivré en l'érigeant en principe, vous avez accepté de détruire les oeuvres de l'homme et de lutter contre lui pour achever sa misère essentielle. Et moi, refusant d'admettre ce désespoir et ce monde torturé, je voulais seulement que les hommes retrouvent leur solidarité pour entrer en lutte

> contre leur destin révoltant. . . .
> Pour tout dire, vous avez choisi l'injustice, vous vous êtes mis avec les dieux. . . .
> J'ai choisi la justice au contraire, pour rester fidèle à la terre. (<u>LAA</u>: 240, 241)111

In choosing <u>justice</u>, that is, he <u>cannot</u> but remain faithful to the world, for he sides with <u>man</u> as a part of the world against the "gods" who would <u>destroy</u> it. "Vous vous êtes reposés dans cette épuisante aventure," he protests, "où votre tâche est de <u>mutiler les âmes</u> et de <u>détruire</u> la terre. . . . Votre logique n'était qu'apparente" (<u>LAA</u>: 240-241).112

And so we may say that his condemnation of modern German ideology rejoins Kant's own critique of its progenitors in Herder and Fichte,113 whose "emotions . . . arouse higher expectations than cool judgement would find justified," and whose "allegories are offered as truths."114 But it clearly indicates that for Camus "criticism <u>alone</u>" can no longer "strike a blow at the root of Materialism, Fatalism, . . . Fanaticism, and Superstition,"115 as they have already <u>overtaken</u> it and become "universally injurious"116 in <u>history</u>.117 Far more exacting, then, than that of Immanuel Kant, the "<u>mesure</u>" of Albert Camus is no less than <u>revolt itself</u>. "C'est la révolte qui <u>est</u> la mesure," he writes, "qui l'<u>ordonne</u>, la <u>défend</u> et la <u>recrée à</u> <u>travers</u> l'histoire <u>et</u> <u>ses</u> <u>désordres</u>. . . . La mesure . . . ne peut se vivre que <u>par</u> la révolte. Elle est un <u>conflit</u> <u>con-</u>

stant, perpétuellement suscité et maîtrisé par l'intelligence" (HR: 704).118 It is also what he calls "la séculaire volonté de ne pas subir" (HR: 704),119 the only "will" it _can_ be in what it perceives to be an absurd universe, and so is _itself_ "the most it can hope for," to paraphrase Richard Weaver, "in this waning day of the West."120

Notes

[1] Lev Braun, *Witness of Decline: Albert Camus, Moralist of the Absurd*, pp. 249, 251, 252. See Braun's "Conclusion: Humanism in Our Time," Sec. 1: "Camus and Classical Humanism," pp. 249-255.

[2] "L'Occident ne retrace pas sa vie quotidienne," writes Camus in the *Carnets*. "Il se propose sans arrêt de grandes images qui l'enfièvrent. Il est à leur poursuite. Il veut être Manfred ou Faust, Don Juan ou Narcisse. Mais l'approximation reste toujours vaine. C'est toujours la fièvre d'unité qui entraîne tout" (*CI*: 232).

[3] There are similar definitions of the absurd both elsewhere in *Le Mythe* (*MS*: 113, 117-118) and in *L'Homme Révolté* (*HR*: 415).

[4] The phrase as it appears is from Ernst Cassirer, *The Philosophy of the Enlightenment*, p. 275, and is also used by Peter Gay, *The Enlightenment, An Interpretation: The Rise of Modern Paganism*, pp. 130, 132, 140. Its author, as Gay points out, is Immanuel Kant (pp. 131-132). See *Critique of Pure Reason*, p. 2, n. 1: "Our age is the age of criticism." (On Gay's "criticism," see *supra*, Chapter I, n. 9.) Henri Peyre rightly states that "the throes of death and pangs of birth suffered when the remnants of the feudal order and the absolute monarchies were swept away, in the Age of Enlightenment and of the American and the French Revolutions, were doubtless felt by the contemporaries as acutely as our anguish and our strange mixture of pride and of revulsion at having discovered how absurd is our world as experienced by us today. The difference, however, lies in the universality of our modern crisis, which is no longer limited to a small area of the populated world but embraces the whole planet" ("The Crisis of Modern Man as Seen by André Malraux and Albert Camus," in *Historical and Critical Essays* [Lincoln: Univ. of Nebraska Press, 1968], p. 265). The "universality of our modern crisis," then, is what we now at last perceive to be the absurdity of the human condition. It is not until 1926 and the publication of Malraux's *La Tentation de l'Occident* that, in the words of Patrick Henry, "the key word 'absurdité' has finally been pronounced," but that "with this acknowledgment we have reached the epitome of anti-rationalist thought. . . . Roughly speaking, from the Enlightenment onward, notwithstanding certain obvious exceptions, the history of philosophy has slowly moved in this direction, fi-

nally attaining the summit of the long tradition of anti-Cartesian rationalism" (Voltaire and Camus: The Limits of Reason and the Awareness of Absurdity, pp. 58-59; see also Peyre, op. cit., pp. 269-270).

⁵Quoted in Cassirer, op. cit., p. 14. Our italics.

⁶As Hegel notes, it is during the earliest phase of the Enlightenment that, in the words of Cassirer, "the lust for knowledge, the libido sciendi, . . . is . . . called a necessary quality of the soul as such and restored to its original rights" (op. cit., p. 14; see supra, Chapter I, n. 5, and text).

⁷Immanuel Kant, Critique of Pure Reason, p. 1.

⁸See supra, Chapter I, text to nn. 32, 35, and 36, as well as nn. 33-34, and text. Cf. Carnets II: "La science explique ce qui fonctionne et non ce qui est" (CII: 40).

⁹"At the same time," he writes, "it must be carefully borne in mind that, while we surrender the power of cognizing, we still reserve the power of thinking objects, as things in themselves. For, otherwise, we should require to affirm the existence of an appearance, without something that appears--which would be absurd" (Critique of Pure Reason, p. 16). "The understanding, therefore, by assuming appearances, grants the existence of things in themselves also" (Prolegomena to Any Future Metaphysics, p. 62).

¹⁰Jean-Paul Sartre, L'Etre et le Néant: Essai d'ontologie phénoménologique, Coll. "Bibliothèque des Idées" (Paris: Gallimard, 1943), p. 306. (Hereafter cited as EN in parentheses.) Our translation. "Je ne trouve dans les choses que ce que j'y ai mis."

¹¹Immanuel Kant, Critique of Pure Reason, pp. 10-11, 13.

¹²"Même les épistémologies les plus rigoureuses," notes Camus in Le Mythe, "supposent des métaphysiques" (MS: 130).

¹³Dagobert D. Runes, ed., Dictionary of Philosophy, p. 295. (Art. "Solipsism," by Ledger Wood.) Our italics. (In all fairness to Kant, however, we should point out--as does A. D. Lindsay--that he was obviously not unaware of the problem. Cf., for example, his letter to Marcus Herz in 1772: "On what principle is

based the relation between that in us which is called a representation and the object? If the representation contains nothing but the way in which the subject is affected by the object, then it is easy to see how it might correspond to this object as its effect, and how this determination of our mind could represent something, i.e. have an object. Possible or sensible representations have, therefore, a conceivable relation to objects, and the principles, which are borrowed from the nature of our soul, have a conceivable validity for all things in so far as they are objects of the senses. Similarly, if that in us which is called presentation were active in regard to the object, i.e. if the object was actually through it brought into being, as the thoughts of God are represented as the originals of things, then, too, the conformity of presentations and objects would be understandable. We can, that is, at least understand the possibility of an archetypal intellect on whose intuition things are themselves based --or of an ectypal intellect, which creates the data of its logical activity out of the sensible intuition of the things. But our understanding is neither through its representations the cause of objects [except in conduct when good purposes bring things into being], nor is the object the cause of the representations of the understanding. The pure concepts of the understanding, then, cannot be abstracted from the feelings of the senses: they cannot express the receptivity of presentations through the senses. They must have their source in the nature of the soul, but not so far as it is either affected by objects or brings objects into being" [Quoted in A. D. Lindsay, "Introduction," in Immanuel Kant, Critique of Pure Reason, trans. J. M. D. Meiklejohn, Everyman's Library, No. 1909 (London: J. M. Dent; New York: E. P. Dutton, 1934), pp. xiv-xv].)

[14] Immanuel Kant, Critique of Pure Reason, p. 20. Our italics.

[15] Our italics. Cf. Carnets I: "Dieu--Méditerranée: des constructions--rien de naturel. Nature= équivalence" (CI: 40).

[16] Cf. Jean-Paul Sartre, La Nausée, Coll. "Folio," 46 (Paris: Gallimard, 1938), pp. 178-179, 179-180: "La racine du marronnier s'enfonçait dans la terre, juste au-dessous de mon banc. Je ne me rappelais plus que c'était une racine. Les mots s'étaient évanouis et, avec eux, la signification des choses, leurs modes d'emploi, les faibles repères que les hommes ont tracés à leur surface. . . . Et puis voilà: tout d'un coup,

c'était là, c'était clair comme le jour: l'existence s'était soudain dévoilée. Elle avait perdu son allure inoffensive de catégorie abstraite: c'était la pâte même des choses, cette racine était pétrie dans de l'existence. Ou plutôt la racine, les grilles du jardin, le banc, le gazon rare de la pelouse, tout ça s'était évanoui; la diversité des choses, leur individualité n'était qu'une apparence, un vernis. Ce vernis avait fondu, il restait des masses monstrueuses et molles, en désordre--nues, d'une effrayante et obscène nudité." (Let us also indicate, however, that the entry from the Carnets in the previous note was written in 1936, two years before the publication of La Nausée.)

17"L'apparition," says Sartre, "ne renvoie pas à l'être comme le phénomène kantien au noumène" (EN: 14).

18Our translation. "L'être est. L'être est en soi. L'être est ce qu'il est."

19Our translation. "Il déborde . . . la connaissance qu'on en prend."

20Cf. La Nausée, pp. 177, 181: "Les choses se sont délivrées de leurs noms. Elles sont là, grotesques, têtues, géantes et ça paraît imbécile de les appeler des banquettes ou de dire quoi que ce soit sur elles: je suis au milieu des Choses, les innommables. Seul, sans mots, sans défenses, elles m'environnent, sous moi, derrière moi, au-dessus de moi. Elles n'exigent rien, elles ne s'imposent pas: elles sont là. . . . De trop: c'était le seul rapport que je pusse établir entre ces arbres, ces grilles, ces cailloux. En vain cherchais-je à compter les marronniers, et les situer par rapport à la Velléda, à comparer leur hauteur avec celle des platanes: chacun d'eux s'échappait des relations où je cherchais à l'enfermer, s'isolait, débordait. Ces relations (que je m'obstinais à maintenir pour retarder l'écroulement du monde humain, des mesures, des quantités, des directions) j'en sentais l'arbitraire; elles ne mordaient plus sur les choses. De trop, le marronnier, là en face de moi un peu sur la gauche. De trop, la Velléda. . ."

21Our translation. "L'en-soi n'a pas de secret: il est massif," observes Sartre. "En un sens, on peut le désigner comme une synthèse. Mais c'est la plus indissoluble de toutes: la synthèse de soi avec soi."

22Our translation. "La réalité humaine se saisit dans sa venue à l'existence comme être incomplet." Cf.

Camus: "Et tout m'est étranger, tout, sans un être à moi, sans un lieu où refermer cette plaie" (CI: 201).

[23]Our translation. The original reads as follows: "Le désir est manque d'être, il est hanté en son être le plus intime par l'être dont il est désir." Here Sartre has clearly been influenced by Hegel. Cf. Camus's analysis of The Phenomenology of Mind in L'Homme Révolté: "Ce qui distingue la conscience de soi du monde naturel n'est pas la simple contemplation où elle s'identifie au monde extérieur et s'oublie elle-même, mais le désir qu'elle peut éprouver à l'égard du monde. Ce désir la rappelle à elle-même dans le temps où elle lui montre le monde extérieur comme différent. Dans son désir, le monde extérieur est ce qu'elle n'a pas, et qui est, mais qu'elle veut avoir pour être, et qu'il ne soit plus. La conscience de soi est donc nécessairement désir" (HR: 546). Camus himself echoes this thought in Le Mythe de Sisyphe: "Le désir profond de l'esprit même dans ses démarches les plus évoluées rejoint le sentiment inconscient de l'homme devant son univers: il est exigence de familiarité, appétit de clarté. Comprendre le monde pour un homme, c'est le réduire à l'humain, le marquer de son sceau" (MS: 110). Cf. Sartre: "Ce que le désir veut être, c'est un vide comblé mais qui informe sa réplétion comme un moule informe le bronze qu'on a coulé dedans" (EN: 146).

[24]For example, see supra, text to n. 7, where Kant speaks of reason's "nature," and n. 13, where he refers to the "nature of the soul." Cf. Critique of Pure Reason, p. 453: "There exists in the faculty of reason a natural desire to venture beyond the field of experience, to attempt to reach the utmost bounds of all cognition by the help of ideas alone, and not to rest satisfied, until it has fulfilled its course and raised the sum of its cognitions into a self-subsistent systematic whole" (our italics). "Au XVIIIe siècle, dans l'athéisme des philosophes," writes Sartre, "la notion de Dieu est supprimée, mais non pas pour autant l'idée que l'essence précède l'existence. Cette idée, nous la retrouvons un peu partout: nous la retrouvons chez Diderot, chez Voltaire, et même chez Kant. L'homme est possesseur d'une nature humaine; cette nature humaine, qui est le concept humain, se retrouve chez tous les hommes, ce qui signifie que chaque homme est un exemple particulier d'un concept universel, l'homme; chez Kant, il résulte de cette universalité que l'homme des bois, l'homme de la nature, comme le bourgeois sont astreints à la même définition et possèdent les mêmes qualités de base. Ainsi, là encore, l'essence d'homme précède cette existence historique que nous rencontrons dans la

nature. L'existentialisme athée, que je représente, est plus cohérent. Il déclare que si Dieu n'existe pas, il y a au moins un être chez qui l'existence précède l'essence, un être qui existe avant de pouvoir être défini par aucun concept et que cet être c'est l'homme ou, comme dit Heidegger, la réalité humaine" (L'Existentialisme est un humanisme, Coll. "Pensées" [Paris: Les Editions Nagel, 1968], pp. 20-21; see also Sartre's essay "A propos de l'existentialisme: Mise au point," in Michel Contat and Michel Rybalka, Les Ecrits de Sartre: Chronologie, bibliographie commentée [Paris: Gallimard, 1970], p. 655). (Camus himself, however, will return to the idea of human nature in L'Homme Révolté. "L'homme absurde est . . . dans un cycle désespérant où l'être n'est que ce qu'il paraît," notes André Nicolas. "Camus pourtant n'a pas été sans vouloir rompre ce cycle lorsque dans l'Homme révolté il fait appel à la notion de nature humaine" [Une Philosophie de l'existence: Albert Camus (Paris: Presses Universitaires de France, 1964), p. 185].)

25See supra, Chapter I, n. 13, and text to nn. 13, 21, and 32, as well as n. 33, and text.

26Blaise Pascal, Pensées, pp. 90-91; no. 72. We therefore agree with Eric Werner that "Le Mythe de Sisyphe et L'Etre et le néant sont l'un comme l'autre des livres de tonalité et d'inspiration pascaliennes. Sartre et Camus centrent tous deux leurs propos respectifs sur la question de la finitude humaine: finitude dont l'envers est le désir d'Etre, la nostalgie de l'Absolu" (De la violence au totalitarisme: Essai sur la pensée de Camus et de Sartre, Coll. "Liberté de l'Esprit" [Paris: Calmann-Lévy, 1972], pp. 240-241).

27"Si j'étais arbre parmi les arbres," writes Camus in Le Mythe, "cette vie aurait un sens ou plutôt ce problème n'en aurait point car je ferais partie de ce monde. Je serais ce monde auquel je m'oppose maintenant par toute ma conscience et par toute mon exigence de familiarité. Cette raison si dérisoire, c'est elle qui m'oppose à toute la création" (MS: 136). "C'est que, en effet," says Sartre, "cette totalité [i.e., the desired unity] n'est pas le pur et simple en-soi contingent du transcendant. Ce que la conscience saisit comme l'être vers quoi elle se dépasse, s'il était pur en-soi, coïnciderait avec l'anéantissement de la conscience. Mais la conscience ne se dépasse point vers son anéantissement, elle ne veut pas se perdre dans l'en-soi d'identité à la limite de son dépassement. C'est pour le pour-soi en tant que tel que le pour-soi revendique l'être-en-soi" (EN: 133). See also the last two quotations in n. 23, supra.

[28]See supra, text to n. 14.

[29]Our translation. "Mais cet être qui 'm'investit' de toute part et dont rien ne me sépare," explains Sartre, "c'est précisément rien qui m'en sépare et ce rien, parce qu'il est néant, est infranchissable."

[30]"Three centuries before Heidegger showed, through a learned and laborious exegesis, that Kant's doctrine of the limitations of human reason really rests on the finitude of our human existence," writes William Barrett, "Pascal clearly saw that the feebleness of our reason is part and parcel of the feebleness of our human condition generally" (Irrational Man: A Study in Existential Philosophy, p. 115).

[31]"En tant, en effet, qu'il se fait être dans l'unité d'un même surgissement comme tout ce qui n'est pas l'être, l'être se tient devant lui comme tout ce que le pour-soi n'est pas. La négation originelle, en effet, est négation radicale. Le pour-soi, qui se tient devant l'être comme sa propre totalité, étant lui-même le tout de la négation est négation du tout. Ainsi, la totalité achevée ou monde se dévoile comme constitutive de l'être de la totalité inachevée par qui l'être de la totalité surgit à l'être" (EN: 230).

[32]Our translation. "Nous concéderons que c'est l'être même qui est présent à la conscience dans la connaissance et que le Pour-soi n'ajoute rien à l'Ensoi, sinon le fait même qu'il y ait de l'En-soi" (EN: 269). See supra, text to n. 20.

[33]Our italics. Announcing this revolution in Western thought earlier in Le Mythe, Camus uses the word plus: "Penser," he writes, "ce n'est plus unifier, rendre familière l'apparence sous le visage d'un grand principe. Penser, . . . c'est diriger sa conscience" (MS: 117). Cf. Jean-Paul Sartre, "Une idée fondamentale de la phénoménologie de Husserl: l'intentionnalité," in Situations I (Paris: Gallimard, 1947), pp. 29-30, 31: "Nous avons tous lu Brunschvicg, Lalande et Meyerson, nous avons tous cru que l'Esprit-Araignée attirait les choses dans sa toile, les couvrait d'une bave blanche et lentement les déglutissait, les réduisait à sa propre substance. Qu'est-ce qu'une table, un rocher, une maison? Un certain assemblage de 'contenus de conscience', un ordre de ces contenus. O philosophie alimentaire! Rien ne semblait pourtant plus évident: la table n'est-elle pas le contenu actu-

el de ma perception, ma perception n'est-elle pas l'état présent de ma conscience? Nutrition, assimilation. Assimilation, disait M. Lalande, des choses aux idées, des idées entre elles et des esprits entre eux. Les puissantes arêtes du monde étaient rongées par ces diligentes diastases: assimilation, unification, identification. . . . Contre la philosophie digestive de l'empirio-criticisme, du néo-kantisme, contre tout 'psychologisme', Husserl ne se lasse pas d'affirmer qu'on ne peut pas dissoudre les choses dans la conscience. . . . Connaître, c'est 's'éclater vers', s'arracher à la moite intimité gastrique pour filer, là-bas, par-delà soi, vers ce qui n'est pas soi, là-bas, près de l'arbre et cependant hors de lui, car il m'échappe et me repousse et je ne peux pas plus me perdre en lui qu'il ne se peut diluer en moi: hors de lui, hors de moi. . . . La philosophie de la transcendance nous jette sur la grand-route, au milieu des menaces, sous une aveuglante lumière." (Louis Faucon informs us, however, that "l'analyse de Camus ne doit rien à Sartre: l'Imagination, chap. IV, 'Husserl' [Alcan, 1936] et 'Une idée fondamentale de la phénoménologie de Husserl, l'intentionalité' [N.R.F., 1er janvier 1939], article repris dans Situations I" ["Commentaires, notes et variantes," in Albert Camus, Essais, Bibliothèque de la Pléiade, 183, ed. Roger Quilliot and Louis Faucon (Paris: Gallimard, 1965), 1438].)

34John Macquarrie correctly states that "there is a general style of methodical description that might be called 'phenomenological,' although the person using it may never have read Husserl. It would, I think, be quite proper to use the word phenomenological for many of Kierkegaard's penetrating descriptions, though these are, of course, pre-Husserlian" (Existentialism, Pelican Books [Baltimore: Penguin Books, 1973], p. 9).

35See supra, Chapter I, n. 6, and text.

36"Et ces deux certitudes," says Camus in Le Mythe, "mon appétit d'absolu et d'unité et l'irréductibilité de ce monde à un principe rationnel et raisonnable, je sais encore que je ne puis les concilier" (MS: 136). Cf. Kant, supra, nn. 6-8, and text, as well as Voltaire, Chapter I, n. 13. We therefore agree with Henri Lefebvre that "la rupture avec la conception d'un monde harmonieux s'opéra dès le milieu du XVIIIe siècle. Elle se trouvait virtuellement dans l'oeuvre de Voltaire (Candide), . . . [et] dans celle de Kant" (Le Marxisme, Coll. "Que sais-je?", 300 [Paris: Presses Universitaires de France, 1948], p. 17). We firmly reject, however, his irreconcilable assertion that "l'existentialisme . . . n'est qu'un 'ersatz' tardif et dégénéré de l'individualisme classique," "qu'il en répudie l'optimisme facile," "[mais que] cela ne change en rien l'essentiel, à savoir, l'effort pour tirer une prétendue vérité absolue d'une description de 'l'existence' et de la conscience individuelles" (pp. 11-12; our italics). (See also our critical remarks on Goldmann's similar view of the "facile optimism" of the Enlightenment, supra, Chapter I, nn. 7 and 8.) In any case, we do not believe, as do our Marxist brethren, that the roots of the contemporary crisis are either social or economic (or even "socio-economic"!), but metaphysical.

[37] See supra, nn. 9-10, and text. "Modern philosophy from Descartes onward," says William Barrett, "has asked itself the question: How can the subject really know the object? By the time of Kant (and despite all the advances in physical knowledge since Descartes) the human mind felt itself so estranged from nature that Kant's answer was that the subject can never know the object-in-itself" (op. cit., p. 249; our italics). Cf. supra, text to nn. 14 and 28.

[38] This is what Sartre means when he writes that "the being of an existent is exactly what it appears" (EN: 12). Our translation. "L'être d'un existant, c'est précisément ce qu'il paraît." Cf. La Nausée, p. 137: "Maintenant, je savais: les choses sont tout entières ce qu'elles paraissent--et derrière elles. . . il n'y a rien."

[39] Our translation. "Si nous nous sommes une fois dépris de ce que Nietzsche appelait 'l'illusion des arrière-mondes' et si nous ne croyons plus à l'être-de-derrière-l'apparition," says Sartre, "celle-ci devient, au contraire, pleine positivité, son essence est un 'paraître' qui ne s'oppose plus à l'être, mais qui en est la mesure, au contraire."

[40] "Ainsi," he concludes, "le dehors s'oppose de nouveau au dedans et l'être-qui-ne-paraît-pas à l'apparition" (EN: 13).

[41] "La pensée moderne," says Sartre, "a réalisé un progrès considérable en réduisant l'existant à la série des apparitions qui le manifestent" (EN: 11).

[42] "Il est vrai que les choses se donnent par profils--c'est-à-dire tout simplement par apparitions. Et il est vrai que chaque apparition renvoie à d'autres apparitions," observes Sartre. "Mais chacune d'elles

est déjà à elle toute seule un être transcendant, non une matière impressionnelle subjective--une plénitude d'être, non un manque--une présence, non une absence" (EN: 28).

⁴³See supra, n. 10, and text to nn. 10-13 and 20. Cf. Sartre: "Par là-même, on peut voir que ce qu'on nomme avec Husserl les catégories (unité-multiplicité-rapport de tout à partie--plus et moins--autour--à côté de--à la suite de--premier, second, etc.--un, deux, trois, etc.--dans et hors de--etc., etc.), ne sont que des brassages idéaux des choses, qui les laissent entièrement intactes, sans les enrichir ni les appauvrir d'un iota et qu'elles indiquent seulement l'infinie diversité des manières dont la liberté du pour-soi peut réaliser l'indifférence de l'être" (EN: 241).

⁴⁴Our italics. See also supra, n. 33, and text, as well as n. 41.

⁴⁵On the following page, Camus states that "L'Ethique elle-même, sous l'un de ses aspects, n'est qu'une longue et rigoureuse confidence" (MS: 178), thereby alluding to the work of Spinoza. Louis Faucon informs us, however, that in the manuscript of Le Mythe he clearly alludes to the work of Kant: "Ms., version biffée: la Critique de la raison pure" (op. cit., 1448). Referring in the Carnets to one of Kant's disciples, Camus notes that "pour Schopenhauer: l'existence objective des choses, leur 'représentation' est toujours agréable, tandis que l'existence subjective, le vouloir est toujours douleur" (CII: 223).

⁴⁶"Pourtant toute la science de cette terre ne me donnera rien qui puisse m'assurer que ce monde est à moi," he argues. "Vous me le décrivez et vous m'apprenez à le classer. Vous énumérez ses lois et dans ma soif de savoir je consens qu'elles soient vraies. Vous démontez son mécanisme et mon espoir s'accroît. Au terme dernier, vous m'apprenez que cet univers prestigieux et bariolé se réduit à l'atome et que l'atome lui-même se réduit à l'électron. Tout ceci est bon et j'attends que vous continuiez. Mais vous me parlez d'un invisible système planétaire où des électrons gravitent autour d'un noyau. Vous m'expliquez ce monde avec une image. Je reconnais alors que vous en êtes venus à la poésie: je ne connaîtrai jamais. Ai-je le temps de m'en indigner? Vous avez déjà changé de théorie. Ainsi cette science qui devait tout m'apprendre finit dans l'hypothèse, cette lucidité sombre dans la métaphore, cette incertitude se résout en oeuvre d'art. Qu'avais-je besoin de tant d'efforts?... Je suis

revenu à mon commencement. . . . vous me donnez à choisir entre une description qui est certaine, mais qui ne m'apprend rien, et des hypothèses qui prétendent m'enseigner, mais qui ne sont point certaines. . . . Vouloir, c'est susciter les paradoxes" (MS: 112). There is no question but that, in the words of John Cruickshank, "the criticism of physics offered by Camus has been made before. Goethe is only one of several thinkers who anticipated what Whitehead was to call the fallacy of 'misplaced concreteness'. Such 'misplaced concreteness' confuses the scientist's picture of reality at any historical moment with reality as it really is" (Albert Camus and the Literature of Revolt, Galaxy Books, 43 [New York: Oxford Univ. Press, 1960], pp. 55-56). Patrick Henry is also correct when he says of Camus that "his criticism of scientific pretention, which he finds ultimately bordering on poetry, . . . recalls Voltaire's criticism of Descartes's philosophical pretention in particular and the legendary sobriquets of 'rêveur' and 'poète' that he constantly levelled at the author of the Discours de la méthode" (op. cit., pp. 60, 61). But neither Henry nor Cruickshank recognizes that the argument is clearly Pascalian. Cf. Pensées, pp. 87-93, passim, no. 72; and supra, n. 26, and text to nn. 25-27. Cf. also Lester G. Crocker, who rightly states that "[Voltaire] does not go so far as Malraux, Camus, or Sartre. . . . He sees [the world], is frightened by it, and dares not contemplate it too long and steadily, or without the defensive weapons of humor and irony" (Nature and Culture: Ethical Thought in the French Enlightenment [Baltimore: The Johns Hopkins Press, 1963], p. 347).

[47]Our italics. Let us note here our agreement with André Nicolas, for whom "les preuves apportées par Camus, en faveur de l'absurde, se dirigent contre l'entendement au sens kantien et non contre la raison, contre le concept ou catégorie formelle et non contre l'idée" (op. cit., pp. 49-50; in this connection, however, see also his critique of Camus, pp. 53-54, n. 1).

[48]Cf. supra, nn. 17-19, 22-23, 27, and 29, and text to nn. 17-19, 21-23, and 28-29. In his essay on Camus's first novel, L'Etranger, the author of L'Etre et le Néant refers with obvious approval to the idea of absurdity in Le Mythe, defining it in the following terms: "L'absurdité . . . manifeste avant tout un divorce: le divorce entre les aspirations de l'homme vers l'unité et le dualisme insurmontable de l'esprit et de la nature, entre l'élan de l'homme vers l'éternel et le caractère fini de son existence, entre le 'souci' qui est son essence même et la vanité de ses efforts"

("Explication de L'Etranger," in Situations I [Paris: Gallimard, 1947], p. 93).

[49]Cf., for example, the following entry from the Carnets: "Répéter ce monde c'est peut-être le trahir plus sûrement qu'en le transfigurant. La meilleure des photographies est déjà une trahison" (CII: 108). This idea reappears in L'Homme Révolté (HR: 672, 673) and in the second Discours de Suède (DS: 1086).

[50]Our italics.

[51]Apostolos Makrakis, The City of Zion, or The Church Built Upon the Rock, i.e., The Human Society in Christ, trans. Denver Cummings (Chicago: The Orthodox Christian Educational Society, 1958), p. 52.

[52]ΕΝ ΑΡΧΗ ΗΝ Ο ΛΟΓΟΣ, ΚΑΙ Ο ΛΟΓΟΣ ΗΝ ΠΡΟΣ ΤΟΝ ΘΕΟΝ, ΚΑΙ ΘΕΟΣ ΗΝ Ο ΛΟΓΟΣ. ΟΥΤΟΣ ΗΝ ΕΝ ΑΡΧΗ ΠΡΟΣ ΤΟΝ ΘΕΟΝ. ΠΑΝΤΑ ΔΙ ΑΥΤΟΥ ΕΓΕΝΕΤΟ, ΚΑΙ ΧΩΡΙΣ ΑΥΤΟΥ ΕΓΕΝΕΤΟ ΟΥΔΕ ΕΝ, Ο ΓΕΓΟΝΕΝ. ΕΝ ΑΥΤΩ ΖΩΗ ΗΝ, ΚΑΙ Η ΖΩΗ ΗΝ ΤΟ ΦΩΣ ΤΩΝ ΑΝΘΡΩΠΩΝ. ΚΑΙ ΤΟ ΦΩΣ ΕΝ ΤΗ ΣΚΟΤΙΑ ΦΑΙΝΕΙ, ΚΑΙ Η ΣΚΟΤΙΑ ΑΥΤΟ ΟΥ ΚΑΤΕΛΑΒΕΝ (ΘΕΙΟΝ ΚΑΙ ΙΕΡΟΝ ΕΥΑΓΓΕΛΙΟΝ ΚΑΤΑ ΙΩΑΝΝΗΝ, ΚΕΦΑΛΑΙΟΝ Α', ΘΕΙΟΝ ΚΑΙ ΙΕΡΟΝ ΕΥΑΓΓΕΛΙΟΝ ΚΑΙ Η ΑΠΟΚΑΛΥΨΙΣ ΙΩΑΝΝΟΥ, ΜΕΤΑ ΠΡΟΣΘΗΚΗΣ ΚΑΙ ΤΟΥ ΚΑΤΑ ΣΩΦΡΟΝΙΟΝ ΒΙΟΥ ΤΩΝ ΕΥΑΓΓΕΛΙΣΤΩΝ, ΕΚ ΤΗΣ ΕΛΛΗΝΙΚΗΣ ΤΥΠΟΓΡΑΦΙΑΣ ΤΟΥ ΑΓΙΟΥ ΓΕΩΡΓΙΟΥ, 1850, p. 271).

[53]Cf. his Métaphysique chrétienne et Néoplatonisme: "Or il n'y a pas d'unité sans forme et sans logos, le logos étant justement le principe d'unité" (ESS: 1272).

[54]See supra, Chapter I, text to n. 6.

[55]Romans 1: 20 reads as follows: "For the invisible things of him from the creation of the world are clearly seen, being understood by the things that are made, even his eternal power and Godhead; so that they are without excuse." Cf. the Orthodox theologian, Paul Evdokimov: "Formerly the sacred was a sign formed by the matter of this world and reflecting a 'wholly other', translating this and testifying to its presence by means of the sign. Does this 'wholly other' speak to man today? For him the transcendent no longer transcends anything; it has lost all correspondence with the real. It is non-existent" (The Struggle With God, trans. Sister Gertrude, S.P., Exploration Books [Glen Rock, N.J.: Paulist Press, 1966], p. 4).

[56]Cf. Carnets I: "Ma vraie philosophie est qu'un quart d'heure après ma mort, je ne serai plus en vie"

(CI: 185). Cf. also Meursault in L'Etranger: "Pour la troisième fois, j'ai refusé de recevoir l'aumônier. Je n'ai rien à lui dire, je n'ai pas envie de parler, je le verrai bien assez tôt. Ce qui m'intéresse en ce moment, c'est d'échapper à la mécanique, de savoir si l'inévitable peut avoir une issue. . . . Mais tout bien considéré, rien ne me permettait ce luxe, tout me l'interdisait, la mécanique me reprenait" (E: 1202, 1203).

[57]Cf. supra, text to n. 47, and n. 48. "Le simple 'souci,'" he says elsewhere in Le Mythe, "est à l'origine de tout" (MS: 107). For Camus as for Heidegger, then, the character of Kant's "pure reason" is even more restricted than he believed. (See supra, n. 24, and text to nn. 24-29.)

[58]See supra, Chapter I, nn. 6, 26, 28-29, and 36, and text to nn. 26-39; and nn. 33, 46, and 47, and text to nn. 2-3, 33, and 44-47 of the present chapter. "Hegel a bien vu," he writes in L'Homme Révolté, "que la philosophie des lumières a voulu délivrer l'homme de l'irrationnel" (HR: 539). But later in the same work he criticizes "l'hostilité de Hegel aux moralistes et . . . son seul axiome [qui] est de vivre conformément aux moeurs et aux coutumes de sa nation. Maxime de conformisme social dont Hegel, en effet, a donné les preuves les plus cyniques" (HR: 550). (For more on Camus's critique of Hegelian historicism, see supra, Chapter I, nn. 6 and 18.) Except for his use of the term "deification," therefore, we agree with John Cruickshank that "Camus criticizes the attempts by . . . different writers to suppress the absurd by rejecting reason and cultivating their own individual forms of what he holds to be irrationality. At the same time, however, he remains on his guard against that deification of reason to which his own tradition is prone" (op. cit., p. 45).

[59]"Et cependant la raison a son ordre où elle est efficace," says André Nicolas of reason in Camus. "Mais d'où vient-elle et à quelles conditions est-elle efficace? Elle n'est pas donnée comme les catégories de l'entendement kantien, elle n'est pas efficace à l'endroit où la situe Kant, encore que son rôle soit aussi d'organiser" (op. cit., p. 51; our italics). In this connection, see also our parallel between Camus and Kant, supra, Chapter I, n. 38, and text to nn. 31-38.

[60]Cf. Martha in Le Malentendu, a woman for whom "ce monde n'est pas raisonnable. . . . Oui," she

cries, "j'en ai assez de porter toujours mon âme, j'ai hâte de trouver ce pays où le soleil tue les questions. Ma demeure n'est pas ici. . . . Je suis restée, petite et sombre, dans l'ennui, enfoncée au coeur du continent et j'ai grandi dans l'épaisseur des terres. . . . J'ai pour patrie ce lieu clos et épais où le ciel est sans horizon. . . . je suis lasse à mourir de cet horizon fermé, et je sens que je ne pourrai pas y vivre un mois de plus. . . . J'imagine avec délices cet autre pays où l'été écrase tout, où les pluies d'hiver noient les villes et où, enfin, les choses sont ce qu'elles sont. . . . Oh! je hais ce monde où nous en sommes réduits à Dieu. . . . Comprenez que . . . pour nous, ni dans la vie ni dans la mort, il n'est de patrie ni de paix. . . . Car on ne peut appeler patrie, n'est-ce pas, cette terre épaisse, privée de lumière" (<u>MAL</u>: 168, 120, 167-168, 170, 142-143, 150, 171, 178).

61This "non-<u>garantie des valeurs</u>," says Claude-Edmonde Magny, is "a philosophical shock compared to which the discovery in the eighteenth century of the plurality of worlds, in the nineteenth of the evolution of species, were as nothing. The Kantian critique has taken more than a century to attain the final development of its philosophical consequences. One must admit that it has succeeded with remarkable thoroughness" (Quoted in Philip Thody, <u>Albert Camus</u>: <u>A Study of His Work</u>, Evergreen Books, 143 [New York: Grove Press, 1959], p. 133). Camus, however, would probably have said of Kant what he did say of Rousseau in another, but similar context: "Rousseau, bien entendu," he asserts, "ne l'aurait pas voulu" (<u>HR</u>: 523).

62Caligula here bears a striking resemblance to Sade, of whom Camus says in <u>L'Homme Révolté</u> that "Sade médite l'attentat contre la création," and from one of whose works he then proceeds to quote as follows: "'J'abhorre la nature. . . Je voudrais déranger ses plans, contrecarrer sa marche, arrêter la roue des astres, bouleverser les globes qui flottent dans l'espace, détruire ce qui la sert, protéger ce qui lui nuit, l'insulter en un mot dans ses oeuvres, et je n'y puis réussir.' . . . 'Nous pourrions peut-être attaquer le soleil, en priver l'univers ou nous en servir pour embraser le monde, ce serait des crimes, cela. . .'" (<u>HR</u>: 455). This repudiation of all being is echoed by Clamence in <u>La Chute</u> when he states that "jusque dans le détail de la vie, j'avais besoin d'être au-dessus" (<u>CH</u>: 1487), and by the character Nada in the following lines from <u>L'Etat de siège</u>: "A mort le monde! Ah, si je pouvais l'avoir tout entier devant moi, comme un taureau qui tremble de toutes ses pattes, avec ses petits yeux brûlants de haine et son mufle rose où la bave met une dentelle sale! Aïe! Quelle minute. Cette vieille main n'hésiterait pas et le cordon de la moelle serait tranché d'un coup et la lourde bête foudroyée tomberait jusqu'à la fin des temps à travers d'interminables espaces! . . . J'ai du mépris jusqu'à la mort. Et rien de cette terre, ni roi, ni comète, ni morale, ne seront jamais au-dessus de moi! . . . Je suis au-dessus de toutes choses, ne désirant plus rien" (ES: 195, 196). They desire nothing, that is, short of becoming God.

63 Our italics. Cf. the revolutionary Stepan in Les Justes: "Il y a trop à faire; il faut ruiner ce monde de fond en comble. . . . L'innocence? Je la connais peut-être. Mais j'ai choisi de l'ignorer et de la faire ignorer à des milliers d'hommes pour qu'elle prenne un jour un sens plus grand" (J: 355, 339).

64 Cf. Carnets II: "Rien n'est pur, rien n'est pur voilà le cri qui a empoisonné ce siècle" (CII: 202). This may well have been its very intention.

65 Camus here quotes from Dostoevsky's The Brothers Karamazov.

66 This explains Camus's incredulousness at a statement of one of his literary predecessors, "Gide: L'athéisme seul peut pacifier le monde aujourd'hui (!)" (CII: 320).

67 Camus then proceeds to quote Marx as follows: "'La philosophie ne peut se réaliser sans la disparition du prolétariat, le prolétariat ne peut se libérer sans la réalisation de la philosophie', et encore: 'Le prolétariat ne peut exister que sur le plan de l'histoire mondiale. . . L'action communiste ne peut exister qu'en tant que réalité historique planétaire'" (HR: 610).

68 See also supra, n. 63. "En face d'une future réalisation de l'idée," observes Camus, "la vie humaine peut être tout ou rien. Plus est grande la foi que le calculateur met dans cette réalisation, moins vaut la vie humaine. A la limite, elle ne vaut plus rien" (HR: 576). This idea first appears in an essay of 1948, "Les Meurtriers délicats." There he adds that "nous sommes aujourd'hui à la limite, c'est-à-dire au temps des bourreaux philosophes" (TRN: 1832).

69 Cf. Stepan: "Je n'aime pas la vie, mais la justice qui est au-dessus de la vie" (J: 320).

[70] Here in the <u>Carnets</u> Camus is quoting Maritain, according to whom, he says, "l'athéisme révolté (l'athéisme absolu) met l'histoire à la place de Dieu et remplace la révolte par une soumission absolue" (<u>CII</u>: 298).

[71] Cf. his important essay, "L'Exil d'Hélène," in <u>L'Eté</u>: "Dieu mort, il ne reste que l'histoire et la puissance" (<u>ETE</u>: 855).

[72] Cf. <u>L'Homme Révolté</u>: "'Si le socialisme, dit un essayiste libertaire, est un éternel devenir, ses moyens sont sa fin.' . . . Ernestan: <u>Le Socialisme et la Liberté</u>" (<u>HR</u>: 628).

[73] See also <u>supra</u>, Chapter I, text to n. 29.

[74] Cf. <u>supra</u>, Chapter I, n. 24.

[75] On the other hand, "celle qui se tourne contre toute histoire enlèv[e] à l'homme le moyen . . . de vivre. . . . [elle le pousse] au 'comment vivre'" (<u>HR</u>: 651). Here, within the ethical realm, we have an example of that Camus who, in the words of Cruickshank, "remains on his guard against that deification of reason to which his own tradition is prone" (see <u>supra</u>, n. 58). "La morale," he writes, "quand elle est formelle, dévore. . . . les juristes bourgeois du XVIIIe siècle, en écrasant sous leurs principes les justes et vivantes conquêtes de leur peuple, ont préparé les deux nihilismes contemporains: celui de l'individu et celui de l'Etat" (<u>HR</u>: 532, 539). We take issue, however, with Roger Quilliot's contention that "à aucun moment, on ne . . . voit [Camus] se passionner pour les écrivains du XVIIIe siècle" ("Commentaires, notes et variantes," in Albert Camus, <u>Essais</u>, Bibliothèque de la Pléiade, 183, ed. Roger Quilliot and Louis Faucon [Paris: Gallimard, 1965], 1317). On the contrary, his passion was for its moralists, many of whom foresaw the dangers of an all too formal ethics. "La vertu absolue est impossible," he remarks, "la république du pardon amène par une logique implacable la république des guillotines. Montesquieu avait déjà dénoncé cette logique comme l'une des causes de la décadence des sociétés, disant que l'abus de pouvoir est plus grand lorsque les lois ne le prévoient pas" (<u>HR</u>: 533).

[76] In this connection, see also <u>supra</u>, Chapter I, n. 6, and text to nn. 21-24. We strongly disagree with him, however, when he then goes on to say of historical reason that therefore "[elle] rappelle parfois la systématisation de l'obsédé, l'affirmation mystique du

verbe, d'autres fois" (HR: 625). We should surely have informed him that insofar as it places "l'affirmation mystique du verbe" in the same category with what he calls "la systématisation de l'obsédé," his statement is a contradiction in terms. As Orthodox, and in contradistinction to the enlightened adversaries of historicism, we do not see the latter as a logical outgrowth of Christianity. One cannot be obsessed (Lat. obsessus, "taken over") by the divine Logos, for if, in the words of Makrakis, we "imagine God to be a perfect will accompanied by perfect wisdom and by perfect power . . . it is logical . . . to infer that He has a mind to substantify a similar being that will have an independent will accompanied by the same divine wisdom and power--as though He had said: 'I am going to create a being to whom I will give my Logos (or my Reason) and my Spirit as free gifts, and who shall be in no respect inferior to me. I am going to produce a free being who shall have as his law of action the very same Logos (or Reason) whom I myself have'" (op. cit., p. 40; our italics). But precisely as the free being which he is, man can choose to accept or to reject this law of action. Irrational, then, is the mind that chooses to reject it. And indeed irrational, says Vladimir Lossky, is "our mind"--not only the historical mind, we may add, but the modern mind itself, which was born, not of Christianity, but of the very Enlightenment that painfully foresaw it as a consequence of its own procedure--a mind "which, owing to the fall, has become 'Kantian', and is always ready to push back everything which transcends the laws, or rather the habits of fallen nature, into the noumenal realm, that of 'objects of faith'" (The Mystical Theology of the Eastern Church [London: James Clarke, 1957], p. 230; our italics). Who, then, are the obsessed, or rather, the possessed?

77See the second of his "Deux Réponses à Emmanuel d'Astier de la Vigerie," in Actuelles I (AI: 364-368). Cf. the quotation from the first of his "Deux Réponses," supra, Chapter I, n. 29.

78See the interview, "Rencontre avec Albert Camus" (ESS: 1337-1343), where he further states that "nous vivons dans leur Europe, l'Europe qu'ils ont faite" (ESS: 1341). See also L'Homme Révolté, where he observes that "le rêve prophétique de Marx et les puissantes anticipations de Hegel ou de Nietzsche ont fini par susciter, après que la cité de Dieu eut été rasée, un Etat rationnel ou irrationnel, mais dans les deux cas terroriste" (HR: 583). We may add, therefore, that the enumeration of authors at the beginning of the text

to this note is in no way arbitrary. Camus reminds us
that Feuerbach is indebted to Hegel, while Marx is indebted to both Hegel and Feuerbach: "De la formule ambiguë de Hegel: 'Dieu sans l'homme n'est pas plus que
l'homme sans Dieu', ses successeurs vont tirer des conséquences décisives. . . . A la fin Feuerbach (que
Marx tenait pour un grand esprit et dont il se reconnaîtra le disciple critique), dans l'Essence du christianisme, remplacera toute théologie par une religion
de l'homme et de l'espèce, qui a converti une grande
partie de l'intelligence contemporaine" (HR: 553).
Spengler, in turn, owes a great deal to both Marx and
Nietzsche, of whom Camus says that "Nietzsche, du moins
dans sa théorie de la surhumanité, Marx avant lui avec
la société sans classes, remplacent tous deux l'au-delà
par le plus tard. . . . Passée au creuset de la philosophie nietzschéenne, la révolte, dans sa folie de liberté, aboutit au césarisme biologique ou historique"
(HR: 488, 489). Cf. Spengler, who includes Feuerbach
as well as Marx and Nietzsche in a list of those authors whose works he considers to be the "real landmarks" of nineteenth-century philosophy: "The actual
and effective philosophy of the 19th Century, then, has
as its one genuine theme the Will-to-Power. It considers this Will-to-Power in civilized-intellectual, ethical, or social forms and presents it as will-to-life,
as life-force, as practical-dynamical principle, as
idea, and as dramatic figure. . . . The real landmarks
are these: . . . 1841. . . . Feuerbach, Das Wesen des
Christenthums. . . . 1847. Marx, Misère de la Philosophie (synthesis of Hegel and Malthus). . . . 1883.
Nietzsche, Also sprach Zarathustra; the Will-to-Power,
but in Romantic disguise" (Form and Actuality, Vol. I
of The Decline of the West, p. 373). (On Spengler and
Hegel, see our own remark as well as that of Judith N.
Shklar, supra, Chapter I, n. 20, and text.) We therefore agree with Jean Sarocchi when he says that "[Camus] est rebelle à la pensée hégélienne et, plus généralement, à toute doctrine historisante; l'évolutionnisme ne l'a pas marqué . . . ; il a été fort sévère
pour le marxisme" (Camus, p. 19).

79Our italics. See his "Quatrième Lettre" (LAA:
239-243).

80Our italics.

81Indeed, if the world has no meaning, then neither does "history," so that the sense of the following
entry from the Carnets is clear: "Quand le détail est
une vie humaine, il est pour moi le monde entier et
toute l'histoire" (CII: 164). In this connection, the

view of Raymond Polin that "Albert Camus's nihilism [sic] attests a kind of harsh, cold rage," that "it resembles a denunciation directed against the meaning of values rather than against their metaphysical essence—a denunciation of the absurdity of all the values scattered in an absurd universe, in a chaotic world where chance is king—a denunciation of a world where out of the anarchy of values is born their equivalence and their nonbeing is confirmed; where everything is given, where there is, consequently, no room for values and ideals, where thoughts as well as lives are deprived of a future" ("The Philosophy of Values in France," in Philosophic Thought in France and the United States: Essays Representing Major Trends in Contemporary French and American Philosophy, ed. Marvin Farber [Buffalo: Univ. of Buffalo Publications in Philosophy, 1950], p. 211; our italics)—is, quite simply, a misreading of Camus (see his bibliography, the same as that of Robert Campbell, "Existentialism in France since the Liberation," ibid., p. 150). To say as much of Camus is to confuse him with Caligula, who in despair of the world seeks refuge in history. "A l'histoire, Caligula," he cries, "à l'histoire" (CAL: 108), thus indicating that if there is anything whose roots can be traced to nihilism, it is modern historicist ideology.

[82] Our italics. See the essay, "Prométhée aux enfers" (ETE: 839-844).

[83] Immanuel Kant, Kant: Selections, ed. Theodore Meyer Greene, Lyceum Editions: Philosophy Series, 307 (New York: Charles Scribner's Sons, 1957), p. 319.

[84] Our italics.

[85] Kant, Selections, p. 309.

[86] Our italics. See also Kant, Selections, p. 320: "This principle: So act in regard to every rational being (thyself and others), that he may always have place in thy maxim as an end in himself, is accordingly essentially identical with this other: Act upon a maxim which, at the same time, involves its own universal validity for every rational being." We may say, in the light of this parallel between the imperatives of Camus and Kant, that we are incredulous at Jean Sarocchi's own imperative that there be none. "[Camus]," he declaims, "s'est tenu au plus loin . . . de la philosophie critique: . . . Kant . . . ne l'intéress[e] [pas]" (op. cit., pp. 18, 19; our italics). Yet nothing could have impelled this critic to write that Kant does not interest Camus if not the question of whether he does,

for as everyone knows, and as Edouard Morot-Sir tells us, "il est indiscutable que toute forme de philosophie en France, en notre siècle, est imprégnée de criticisme kantien" (La Pensée française d'aujourd'hui, Coll. "'SUP': Le Philosophe," 100 [Paris: Presses Universitaires de France, 1971], p. 57). And while it is true that "certaines de ces formes ont été plus typiquement kantiennes" (loc. cit.) and that the philosophy of Camus may not be among them, we reaffirm with Lev Braun that the cornerstone of his humanism "coincides with one of Kant's criteria of the ethical act, namely, that man should be regarded as end and not as means" (see supra, Chapter I, n. 35). But even this statement is in need of qualification, and should read: "and not merely as means"; so that the assertion of Jean-Jacques Brochier that "Camus, sans souci d'aucune distinction, oppose l'idéologie . . . à un vécu confus, fait de principes moraux vaguement kantiens (considérer les autres non comme un moyen mais comme une fin)" (Albert Camus, philosophe pour classes terminales [Paris: André Balland, 1970], p. 66; our italics), is, quite simply, one of a "philosophe de classes terminales." For such, and especially for those of the Marxist variety, Kantian principles are vaguely Kantian. And so we refer them--and Brochier--to the sources, to the writings, that is, of both Camus and Kant, but to the following one of Camus as an example: "Quand la fin est absolue, c'est-à-dire, historiquement parlant, quand on la croit certaine, on peut aller jusqu'à sacrifier les autres. Quand elle ne l'est pas, on ne peut sacrifier que soi-même, dans l'enjeu d'une lutte pour la dignité commune. La fin justifie les moyens? Cela est possible. Mais qui justifiera la fin? A cette question, que la pensée historique laisse pendante, la révolte répond: les moyens" (HR: 695-696). And as for Kant, Stephen Toulmin aptly states that, "writing in the late eighteenth century, Immanuel Kant had few serious moral expectations about history; but his own obsessively moderate political liberalism took care not to rule out such hopes on principle" (Allan Janik and Stephen Toulmin, Wittgenstein's Vienna, Touchstone Books [New York: Simon and Schuster, 1973], p. 244). And so the charge of Francis Jeanson against both Camus and his fellow men that "vous vous révoltez, et chacun d'eux comme vous se révolte, mais simultanément et non point ensemble, non point les uns avec les autres," that "cette révolte commune ne vous rend pas solidaires, elle ne désigne qu'une juxtaposition de solitudes" ("Pour tout vous dire," Les Temps Modernes, 8, No. 82 [Aug. 1952], 381), is just as unfounded as that of Brochier. We agree, rather, with Otto Friedrich Bollnow that "on en arrive par [l'enchaînement des idées qui aboutit à la reconnaissance de la mesure] à la reconnaissance que toute liberté trouve sa limite dans la liberté d'autrui. C'est là, précisément, comme on l'a montré ailleurs, le principe dominant de Kant dans le domaine moral" ("Du monde absurde à la pensée de midi: 1] La Peste [1948]; 2] L'Homme révolté [1954]," Configuration Critique d'Albert Camus, II: Camus devant la critique de langue allemande, ed. Richard Thieberger, La Revue des Lettres Modernes, Nos. 90-93 [Winter 1963], p. 68; see also his "Existenzialismus und Ethik," Die Sammlung, 4 [1949], 321-335). In this connection, therefore, the charge of Theodore Ziolkowski that Bollnow "rather patronizingly discussed The Rebel from the position of the professional philosopher," that he "reduces [Camus's] ethical position to a variation on Kant's categorical imperative, and completely ignores the refutation and rejection of the German ideologies" ("Camus in Germany, or the Return of the Prodigal Son," Yale French Studies, No. 25, Albert Camus [Spring 1960], p. 134; our italics), is not only unfounded, but flagrantly unfair to Kant, and based on a widespread misreading of Kant that links him to these ideologies. As K. R. Popper has rightly observed of Kant, "he is only too often claimed to be a forerunner of Hegel; but in view of the fact that he recognized in the romanticism of both Herder and Fichte a doctrine diametrically opposed to his own, this claim is grossly unjust to Kant, and there can be no doubt that he would have strongly resented it. It is the tremendous influence of Hegelianism," says Popper, "that led to a wide acceptance of this, I believe, completely untenable claim" (The Spell of Plato, Vol. I of The Open Society and Its Enemies, p. 247, n. 4; see also pp. 1 and 293, n. 14, as well as The High Tide of Prophecy: Hegel, Marx, and the Aftermath, Vol. II of The Open Society and Its Enemies, pp. 21, 38-41, 44-45, 52-54, 78, 224, 250-251, 393-395, 299, n. 53, 307, n. 19, 308, n. 30, 309, n. 41, 312-313, nn. 57-58, 313-314, n. 62, and 353, n. 4; and supra, Chapter I, n. 18). This dissenting view, however, is not only held by Germans like Popper, but even by Frenchmen like Julien Benda (to whom Popper himself refers in The High Tide of Prophecy, p. 393). Noting that "Kant a toujours flétri la religion de la 'vie'" (Kant, Coll. "Les Classiques de la Liberté," 7 [Geneva: Éditions des Trois Collines, 1948], p. 14, n. 2), Benda goes on to state that "[la morale kantienne] implique la liberté du choix, c'està-dire la faculté pour l'homme d'être immoral avec volonté de ne l'être pas. En quoi la thèse s'oppose: d'une part, à la morale évolutionniste . . . , qui veut que le développement des générations successives dépose automatiquement en nous, avec le temps, les sentiments et modes d'action conformes à la moralité; d'autre part, à la doctrine marxiste, selon laquelle ce résultat sera obtenu par une éducation appropriée; thèses qui, toutes deux, suppriment la volonté dans l'accomplissement de l'acte moral. . . . Son contrepied [aussi] est la doctrine--essentiellement allemande: l'Allemagne moderne vomit le kantisme--qui porte au sommet des valeurs morales la volonté pour l'individu (ou pour une collection d'individus) de se livrer à son besoin d'expansion hors de toute attention du droit d'autrui; c'est La Volonté de Puissance de Nietzsche, L'Unique et sa Propriété de Stirner, le 'dynamisme' du national-socialisme, l'exaltation de la race germanique parce qu'elle est essentiellement une 'volonté d'irruption, de propulsion du dedans vers le dehors', autrement dit de sac du droit des autres" (pp. 14-15, 18-19; see also p. 20, n. 2). And indeed the moral position of Kantianism as Benda here describes it is very close to what we have shown, and to what Jean Sarocchi himself admits to be that of Camus (cf. supra, n. 78, and text). But such evidence does not dissuade an Eric Werner from going even further than Ziolkowski or Sarocchi and asserting, not only that "Camus n'est pas kantien" (op. cit., p. 96), that there is "rien en définitive de plus éloigné du kantisme que l'Homme révolté" (p. 113; our italics), but also "[l'] antikantisme de Camus" (p. 260; our italics). "Par delà Marx," he decrees, "il vise Kant" (p. 114; were they to read it, this statement would even shock Jeanson and Brochier, the first of whom referred to Camus's "'individualisme altruiste'" [art. cit., 381], the second of whom, placing Camus in the same tradition as that of Kant, "ne marquera jamais assez, chez cet héritier de Descartes et du cartésianisme . . . , l'aversion des philosophies de la conscience de soi, de la théorie de l'histoire, et de l'histoire tout court, c'est-à-dire de Hegel et de Marx" [op. cit., p. 65]). Now Camus may well be alluding to Kant, among others, when at one point in L'Homme Révolté he affirms that, "dans le mouvement de révolte tel que nous l'avons envisagé jusqu'ici, on n'élit pas un idéal abstrait, par pauvreté de coeur, et dans un but de revendication stérile. On exige que soit considéré ce qui, dans l'homme, ne peut se réduire à l'idée, cette part chaleureuse qui ne peut servir à rien d'autre qu'à être" (HR: 428). And this is probably due to the influence of Nietzsche and the critique, as Braun says, of "all the formalists whom Nietzsche had in mind when he called Kant, unjustly regarded as their spiritual father, 'the Mongol of Koenigsberg'" (op. cit., p. 137; on the more "emotional" humanism of Camus, see Pierre-Henri Simon's suggestion of a parallel between the latter and Diderot in Présence de Camus, Coll. "La Lettre et l'Esprit" [Brussels: La Renaissance du Livre, 1962], p. 55; and on Camus's critique of his own tradition, see supra, nn. 58 and 75). Yet Camus echoes Kant when in the paragraph of L'Homme Révolté immediately preceding the passage we have quoted he defines revolt as "le mouvement qui dresse l'individu pour la défense d'une dignité commune à tous les hommes" (HR: 428). Kant says no less than this when he affirms that "reason . . . refers every maxim of the will, regarding it as legislating universally, to every other will and also to every action towards oneself; and this . . . from the idea of the dignity of a rational being, obeying no law but that which he himself also gives" (Selections, p. 316). And so Werner's claim that in the section of L'Homme Révolté entitled "Les Régicides" (HR: 530-540) Camus "critique même de façon très ferme le formalisme kantien" (p. 48; our italics) is one that cannot be justified, not only because it fails to note that Camus does not here even mention the name of Kant, but also because it fails to acknowledge Camus's distinction--despite his critique of the lumières--between the latter and those whom he calls "les juristes bourgeois du XVIIIe siècle"--juristes whose "bel édifice, [comme] Montesquieu l'avait déjà vu, ne pouvait se passer de la vertu. La Révolution française, en prétendant bâtir l'histoire sur un principe de pureté absolue, ouvre les temps modernes en même temps que l'ère de la morale formelle" (HR: 539, 531). And Julien Benda need not remind us, quoting from L'Esprit des lois, that "on saisit ici la justesse de la distinction de Montesquieu entre les systèmes qui 'ont la liberté politique pour objet' et ceux 'qui ne tendent qu'à la gloire des citoyens, de l'Etat et du Prince'. Kant opte résolument pour les premiers" (op. cit., p. 38; see also Camus's other reference to Montesquieu from the section cited, supra, n. 75). But even Werner admits that "Kant . . . rapproche, dans la Critique de la faculté de juger, la notion politique de république de la notion biologique d'organisation: 'En effet, dans un tel tout, chaque membre ne doit pas seulement être moyen, mais aussi en même temps fin, et tandis qu'il contribue à la possibilité du tout, il doit à son tour, en ce qui concerne sa place et sa fonction, être déterminé par l'Idée du tout.' La conception camusienne de la coexistence sociale correspond très exactement à cette définition que donne Kant de la République. Pour Kant, l'idéal est en définitive, non pas la totalité (c'est-à-dire l'abolition des différences), mais l'unité (c'est-à-dire l'intégration de ces différences). On ne doit pas chercher à dissoudre les individualités, mais à les organiser. . . . la pensée politique de Camus se situ[e] directement dans la tradition 'républicaine' (au sens kantien du mot): Camus ne postule pas l'abolition des différences, mais leur intégration" (pp. 106, 163). On this note we conclude our polemic on Camus and Kant.

[87]"Ces remarques," notes Camus of statements like the one we have quoted from Le Mythe, "n'ont rien d'original" (MS: 107). "Toute réflexion un peu radicale," writes Emmanuel Mounier, "commence par ce pseudo-nihilisme: Descartes aussi bien que Socrate, Kant que Pascal. Il est par essence provisoire, non seulement en ce qu'il n'est qu'une étape sur une démarche plus longue, mais en ce qu'il regarde en avant, qu'il ouvre la voie à un avenir de valeurs" ("Albert Camus ou l'appel des humiliés," Esprit, 18, No. 1, Les Carrefours de Camus [Jan. 1950], 53-54). In this connection, cf. Kant, supra, Chapter I, n. 35.

[88]Kant, Selections, p. 308. Kant's italics.

[89]See supra, n. 86.

[90]Our italics. The "rock" to which Camus here refers is that of Sisyphus, the mythical figure whose name appears in the title of Le Mythe. Cf. the essay in L'Eté where he refers to both the "rock" and the "vulture" of Prometheus, "Prométhée aux enfers": "Le héros enchaîné maintient dans la foudre et le tonnerre divins sa foi tranquille en l'homme. C'est ainsi qu'il est plus dur que son rocher et plus patient que son vautour" (ETE: 844).

[91]Kant, Selections, p. 316.

[92]Pascal, op. cit., pp. 162-163; no. 347. Cf. no. 365: "Toute la dignité de l'homme consiste en la pensée. La pensée est donc une chose admirable et incomparable par sa nature" (p. 165; our italics).

[93]In this connection, see supra, n. 24. In L'Homme Révolté he definitively opposes what he calls "l'idée (hostile à toute la pensée antique qui, au contraire, se retrouvait en partie dans l'esprit révolutionnaire français) que l'homme n'a pas de nature humaine donnée une fois pour toutes, qu'il n'est pas une créature achevée, mais une aventure dont il peut être en partie le créateur" (HR: 542). And it is here that he opposes Pascal, for whom "la nature n'est pas si uniforme. C'est la coutume qui fait . . . cela, car elle contraint la nature" (op. cit., p. 101; no. 97). On custom, then, Pascal inadvertently anticipates Hegel and modern historicism. (See Camus's critique of cus-

tom in Hegel, supra, n. 58.) Jean-Paul Sartre's remark to Camus, however, that "vous restez dans notre grande tradition classique qui, depuis Descartes et si l'on excepte Pascal, est tout entière hostile à l'Histoire" ("Réponse à Albert Camus," Les Temps Modernes, 8, No. 82 [Aug. 1952], 347; rpt. in Situations IV [Paris: Gallimard, 1964], p. 113; our italics) is one that cannot be justified, for Pascal then goes on to say of custom that "quelquefois la nature la surmonte, et retient l'homme dans son instinct, malgré toute coutume, bonne ou mauvaise" (loc. cit.). More accurate, in our view, is Sartre's statement shortly after the death of Camus that the latter "représentait en ce siècle, et contre l'Histoire, l'héritier actuel de cette longue lignée de moralistes dont les oeuvres constituent peut-être ce qu'il y a de plus original dans les lettres françaises" ("Albert Camus," in Situations IV [Paris: Gallimard, 1964], p. 127). But then he further states that "son humanisme têtu, étroit et pur, austère et sensuel, livrait un combat douteux contre les événements massifs et difformes de ce temps" (loc. cit.; our italics), thereby responding, as he had done so at length in his previous article, to the charge of Camus in L'Homme Révolté that "nos existentialistes . . . [sont] . . . soumis eux aussi, pour le moment, à l'historisme et à ses contradictions" (HR: 651).

[94] Our italics.

[95] Our italics.

[96] Our italics.

[97] Our italics. He is as fully aware as Sartre, however, that one cannot logically justify the idea of a human nature without that of a God as its author (see supra, n. 24). "Mais s'il y a une nature humaine," he asks in the Carnets, "d'où vient-elle" (CII: 184)? But for him it is clear that if there were no human nature there would be no reason for revolt.

[98] "Qu'est-ce que l'homme?" asks Camus in the second of his Lettres à un ami allemand. "Mais là, je vous arrête, car nous le savons. Il est cette force qui finit toujours par balancer les tyrans et les dieux. Il est la force de l'évidence. C'est l'évidence humaine que nous avons à préserver. . . . Si rien n'avait de sens, vous seriez dans le vrai. Mais il y a quelque chose qui garde du sens" (LAA: 228).

[99] Our italics.

[100] Our italics.

[101] Our italics. In this connection, therefore, and except for his choice of the term "conquest," we agree with Ira O. Wade, who in "seeking the right perspective upon the Enlightenment, . . . has to go back at least to the fourteenth century, when man renounced his faith in divine guidance and providence and set forth upon the conquest of himself and his world, by the use of his intellectual powers. . . . Briefly stated the whole epoch from 1348 (the plague of Florence) to 1948 (Camus' La Peste) forms an organic whole when man dared proclaim his ability to make his world and accept his responsibility for this act of revolt" (The Intellectual Origins of the French Enlightenment [Princeton: Princeton Univ. Press, 1971], pp. 61, 62). We disagree with him, however, when he then goes on to say that man invariably dared to do so "with remarkable naïvety" (p. 62).

[102] Our italics.

[103] See supra, Chapter I, nn. 6, 10, 18, 19, 24-25, 30, and 35, and text to nn. 24-25 and 34-37.

[104] Gay, op. cit., pp. 81, 82. Our italics.

[105] See supra, text to n. 14.

[106] See supra, n. 61, and text, as well as n. 86.

[107] See supra, n. 47, and text, as well as our parallel between Camus and Kant, Chapter I, text to n. 36.

[108] "Il ne reconnaissait pas, peut-être, de droits souverains au raisonnement," writes Brice Parain of Camus. "Il voulait des enchaînements de faits, ce qu'on appelle maintenant des situations. . . . Mais c'est par là, je crois, qu'il a été lié si intimement au monde d'aujourd'hui, qu'il en est devenu l'un des symboles. Il avait conservé presque tout de notre tradition classique, le besoin d'une morale, le culte du travail et de la volonté, la pudeur, le goût de l'économie, . . . sauf, donc, sa structure, disons, mathématisante, la croyance au monde intelligible du genre platonicien" ("Un héros de notre temps," La Nouvelle Revue Française, 8, No. 87, Hommage à Albert Camus [March 1960], 407; our italics). Cf. the first epigraph to the present chapter, from L'Envers et l'Endroit (EE: 44).

[109] Our italics. Cf. Noces: "Le monde finit tou-

jours par vaincre l'histoire" (N: 65).

110 See supra, text to n. 75. Cf. Victor Brombert's article on Camus's short story in L'Exil et le Royaume, "Le Renégat ou Un esprit confus" (ER: 1577-1593): "The missionary who reneges on his mission does so because his thirst for a despotic ideal can only find satisfaction in evil. For evil, unlike good, can be absolute in human terms. The Renegade, seeing that good is a constantly postponed and tiring project, refuses to pursue any further an ever receding boundary. He knows that the Reign of Goodness is impossible. So he turns to the Reign of Evil as to the only abstraction that can be translated into a flawless truth. . . . The conversion, to be sure, leads to a denial of all values. . . . But this is the price to pay: the militant need for absolute affirmation implies absolute negation. Ideology replaces life" ("'The Renegade' or the Terror of the Absolute," Yale French Studies, No. 25, Albert Camus [Spring 1960], p. 84).

111 The epigraph to his "Quatrième Lettre" is from Obermann by Senancour, a disciple of Rousseau: "L'homme est périssable. Il se peut; mais périssons en résistant, et si le néant nous est réservé, ne faisons pas que ce soit une justice" (LAA: 239)!

112 Our italics.

113 See supra, n. 86. K. R. Popper reminds us that "it [is] Hegel's predecessor, Fichte, . . . who must be credited with the original anti-humanitarian argument. Speaking of the word 'humanity', Fichte wrote: 'If one had presented, to the German, instead of the Roman word "humaneness" its proper translation, the word "manhood", then . . . he would have said: "It is after all not so very much to be a man instead of a wild beast!" . . . Fichte's doctrine is repeated by Spengler, who writes: 'Manhood is either a zoological expression or an empty word'; and also by Rosenberg, who writes: 'Man's inner life became debased when . . . an alien motive was impressed upon his mind: salvation, humanitarianism, and the culture of humanity'" (The High Tide of Prophecy: Hegel, Marx, and the Aftermath, pp. 70-71). Cf. Camus in his fourth Lettre à un ami allemand: "Vous avez supposé qu'en l'absence de toute morale humaine ou divine les seules valeurs étaient celles qui régissaient le monde animal, c'est-à-dire la violence et la ruse. Vous en avez conclu que l'homme n'était rien et qu'on pouvait tuer son âme, que dans la plus insensée des histoires la tâche d'un individu ne pouvait être que l'aventure de la puissance, et sa morale,

le réalisme des conquêtes" (LAA: 240). In this connection, see also Camus's remark on Feuerbach, supra, Chapter I, n. 24.

[114] Quoted in Popper, The High Tide of Prophecy, p. 53.

[115] Immanuel Kant, Critique of Pure Reason, p. 20. Our italics. (See supra, text to n. 14.)

[116] Loc. cit.

[117] See Camus's critique of Hegel, with our comments, supra, Chapter I, n. 6.

[118] Our italics. "Il faut donc bien," he says earlier in L'Homme Révolté, "que la révolte tire ses raisons d'elle-même, puisqu'elle ne peut les tirer de rien d'autre. Il faut qu'elle consente à s'examiner pour apprendre à se conduire" (HR: 419-420).

[119] Here he is actually referring to revolt.

[120] Richard M. Weaver, Ideas Have Consequences, Phoenix Books, 44 (Chicago: Univ. of Chicago Press, 1948), p. 187. The same, therefore, may be said of the work of Camus what he himself says of the work of Roger Martin du Gard: "Son oeuvre est aussi celle du doute, de la raison déçue et persévérante, de l'ignorance reconnue et du pari sur l'homme sans autre avenir que lui-même" (ESS: 1132).

SELECT BIBLIOGRAPHY

This bibliography is divided into four sections. The first, entitled "Primary Sources," consists of those works by Camus which we have specifically consulted in the writing of this essay. They include most of his major works collected in Théâtre, Récits, Nouvelles (ed. Roger Quilliot [Paris: Gallimard, 1962], 2090pp.) and in Essais (ed. Roger Quilliot and Louis Faucon [Paris: Gallimard, 1965], 1975pp.), as well as certain of those items appearing in the "Textes complémentaires" at the end of each of these two volumes (pp. 1687-2082, passim, and pp. 1167-1930, passim, respectively). Added to the list of entries drawn from the collected works are Camus's notebooks, also edited by Quilliot and separately published as Carnets I (Paris: Gallimard, 1962) and Carnets II (Paris: Gallimard, 1964). We have used two different texts of Camus's last interview, both of which are abridged reprints of the original published in Venture (Dec. 20, 1959): "La dernière interview," in Paul Ginestier, Pour connaître la pensée de Camus (Paris: Bordas, 1964) and "Dernière interview d'Albert Camus," in Essais. Each text contains portions omitted in the other, and so we include them both in our list of primary sources. The second section, entitled "Bibliographical Sources," is a list of four bibliographies, three of which have proven invaluable as tools of research in secondary sources: the works of Fitch and Hoy and of Roeming on Camus, and of François and Claire Lapointe on Sartre, with a list of comparative studies in Sartre and Camus. To these we add Les Ecrits de Sartre by Contat and Rybalka, an excellent bibliography of Sartre's writings containing important information on the relationship of his thought to that of Camus. The third section, entitled "Secondary Sources," consists almost exclusively of books and articles directly or indirectly relating to Camus as moralist and philosopher. With three exceptions, they are in English and French. We believe them to be among the most significant studies written on this subject to date. The fourth and last section, entitled "Other Works Consulted," is a list of books and articles which have been especially helpful in our analysis of Camus's thought.

I. Primary Sources

Camus, Albert. "'A lire attentivement la presse parisienne . . .' (Combat, 23 novembre 1944)." Essais. Bibliothèque de la Pléiade, 183. Ed. Roger Quilliot and Louis Faucon. Paris: Gallimard, 1965, 1540-1541.

_____. Actuelles I: Chroniques 1944-1948. Essais, 245-406.

_____. Actuelles II: Chroniques 1948-1953. Essais, 711-804.

_____. Actuelles III: Chroniques Algériennes, 1939-1958. Essais, 887-999.

_____. "Les Archives de la Peste." Théâtre, Récits, Nouvelles. Bibliothèque de la Pléiade, 161. Ed. Roger Quilliot. Paris: Gallimard, 1962, 1967-1973.

_____. "Au service de l'homme." Essais, 1544-1546.

_____. Caligula. Théâtre, Récits, Nouvelles, 3-108.

_____. Carnets I: mai 1935-février 1942. Collection Soleil, 100. Ed. Roger Quilliot. Paris: Gallimard, 1962, 252pp.

_____. Carnets II: janvier 1942-mars 1951. Collection Soleil, 156. Ed. Roger Quilliot. Paris: Gallimard, 1964, 350pp.

_____. La Chute. Théâtre, Récits, Nouvelles, 1475-1551.

_____. "Conférence prononcée à Athènes sur l'avenir de la tragédie." Théâtre, Récits, Nouvelles, 1701-1711.

_____. "La culture indigène: la nouvelle culture méditerranéenne." Essais, 1321-1327.

_____. "De l'insignifiance." Théâtre, Récits, Nouvelles, 1902-1906.

_____. "Défense de l'Homme révolté." Essais, 1702-1716.

111

_____. "La démocratie exercice de la modestie."
Essais, 1580-1583.

_____. "La dernière interview." In Ginestier,
Paul. Pour connaître la pensée de Camus. Coll.
"Pour connaître la pensée." Paris: Bordas, 1964,
pp. 201-204.

_____. "Dernière interview d'Albert Camus." Essais, 1925-1928.

_____. Discours de Suède. Essais, 1065-1096.

_____. L'Envers et l'Endroit. Essais, 1-50.

_____. L'Etat de siège. Théâtre, Récits, Nouvelles, 181-300.

_____. L'Eté. Essais, 805-886.

_____. L'Etranger. Théâtre, Récits, Nouvelles, 1123-1212.

_____. L'Exil et le Royaume. Théâtre, Récits, Nouvelles, 1553-1686.

_____. "Extraits d'interviews." Théâtre, Récits, Nouvelles, 1879-1881.

_____. "Extraits de lettres à Guy Dumur." Essais, 1668-1671.

_____. "La guerre." Essais, 1376-1377.

_____. "Herman Melville." Théâtre, Récits, Nouvelles, 1907-1911.

_____. "Hommage à un exilé." Essais, 1809-1816.

_____. L'Homme Révolté. Essais, 407-709.

_____. "L'Intelligence et l'Echafaud." Théâtre, Récits, Nouvelles, 1895-1902.

_____. "Interview au Diario de Sao Paulo." Essais, 1697-1699.

_____. "Interview à Servir." Essais, 1427-1429.

_____. "Introduction aux Maximes de Chamfort."
Essais, 1099-1109.

_____. Les Justes. Théâtre, Récits, Nouvelles, 301-393.

_____. "Lettre d'Albert Camus à Roland Barthes sur La Peste." Club, No. 21 (Feb. 1955), p. 7. Rpt. "Lettre à Roland Barthes sur la Peste." Théâtre, Récits, Nouvelles, 1973-1975.

_____. "Lettre à Caliban." Essais, 1563.

_____. "Lettre au directeur des Temps Modernes." Les Temps Modernes, 8, No. 82 (Aug. 1952), 317-333. Rpt. "Révolte et Servitude." Actuelles II. Essais, 754-774.

_____. "Lettre à Monsieur le directeur de la Nef." Théâtre, Récits, Nouvelles, 1745-1746.

_____. "Lettre à Pierre Bonnel." Essais, 1422-1424.

_____. "Lettre au sujet du Parti pris de Francis Ponge." Essais, 1662-1668.

_____. Lettres à un ami allemand. Essais, 213-243.

_____. Le Malentendu. Théâtre, Récits, Nouvelles, 109-180.

_____. Métaphysique chrétienne et Néoplatonisme. Essais, 1224-1313.

_____. "Les Meurtriers délicats." Théâtre, Récits, Nouvelles, 1827-1833.

_____. "Le Mur de Jean-Paul Sartre." Essais, 1419-1422.

_____. Le Mythe de Sisyphe. Essais, 89-211.

_____. "La Nausée de Jean-Paul Sartre." Essais, 1417-1419.

_____. Noces. Essais, 51-88.

_____. "'Non, je ne suis pas existentialiste.'" Essais, 1424-1427.

_____. "Note à Max-Pol Fouchet sur Bériha." Essais, 1206-1207.

_____. "Le parti de la liberté: hommage à Salvador de Madariaga." *Essais*, 1802-1809.

_____. *La Peste*. *Théâtre, Récits, Nouvelles*, 1213-1474.

_____. "La philosophie du siècle." *Essais*, 1203-1205.

_____. "Poème sur la Méditerranée." *Essais*, 1207-1209.

_____. "Portrait d'un élu." *Essais*, 1597-1603.

_____. "Pour Dostoïevski." *Théâtre, Récits, Nouvelles*, 1887-1889.

_____. "Préface." *Théâtre, Récits, Nouvelles*, 1793.

_____. "Préface à l'édition américaine du *Théâtre*." *Théâtre, Récits, Nouvelles*, 1729-1734.

_____. "Prière d'insérer (1944)." *Théâtre, Récits, Nouvelles*, 1744-1745.

_____. "Prière d'insérer (1949)." *Théâtre, Récits, Nouvelles*, 1834-1835.

_____. "Questionnaire pour *Spectacles*." *Théâtre, Récits, Nouvelles*, 1891-1892.

_____. *Réflexions sur la guillotine*. *Essais*, 1019-1064.

_____. "Remarque sur la révolte." *Essais*, 1682-1697.

_____. "Rencontre avec Albert Camus." *Essais*, 1337-1343.

_____. "René Char." *Essais*, 1163-1166.

_____. "Réponse à Domenach." *Essais*, 1751-1758.

_____. "Roger Martin du Gard." *Essais*, 1131-1155.

_____. "Sous le signe de la liberté." *Essais*, 1746-1749.

_____. "Sur les Iles de Jean Grenier." Essais, 1157-1161.

_____. "Sur une philosophie de l'expression de Brice Parain." Essais, 1671-1682.

II. Bibliographical Sources

Fitch, Brian T., and Peter C. Hoy. Albert Camus 1 (3): Essai de bibliographie des études en langue française consacrées à Albert Camus (1937-1970). Calepins de bibliographie, No. 1. Paris: Lettres Modernes, Minard, 1972, 480pp.

Roeming, Robert F. Camus: A Bibliography. Madison: Univ. of Wisconsin Press, 1968, xii-298pp.

Lapointe, François, and Claire Lapointe. Jean-Paul Sartre and His Critics: An International Bibliography (1938-1975). Bibliographies of Famous Philosophers, 2. Bowling Green, Ohio: Philosophy Documentation Center, 1975, iv-447pp.

Contat, Michel, and Michel Rybalka. Les Ecrits de Sartre: Chronologie, bibliographie commentée. Paris: Gallimard, 1970, 788pp.

III. Secondary Sources

Abbou, André. "La pensée d'Albert Camus en question: Entre exégètes et censeurs." Albert Camus 2: Langue et Langage. Ed. Brian T. Fitch. La Revue des Lettres Modernes, Nos. 212-216 (1969), pp. 163-179.

_____. "Contre l'instinct de mort." Albert Camus 4: Sources et Influences. Ed. Brian T. Fitch. La Revue des Lettres Modernes, Nos. 264-270 (1971), pp. 151-169.

Abel, Lionel. "Albert Camus: Moralist of Feeling." Commentary, 31, No. 2 (Feb. 1961), 172-175.

Aiken, Henry David. "The Revolt Against Ideology." Commentary, 37, No. 4 (April 1964), 29-39.

Albérès, René-Marill. "Albert Camus et le mythe de Prométhée." In La Révolte des écrivains d'aujourd'hui. Coll. "Mise au Point." Paris: Corrêa, 1949, pp. 63-81.

_____. "Albert Camus et la nostalgie de l'Eden." In *Les Hommes traqués*. Paris: La Nouvelle Edition, 1953, pp. 187-220.

Alexander, Ian W. "La philosophie existentialiste en France: Ses sources et ses problèmes fondamentaux." *French Studies*, 1, No. 2 (April 1947), 95-114.

Alter, André. "De *Caligula* aux *Justes*: de l'absurde à la justice." *Revue d'Histoire du Théâtre*, 12, No. 4, *Camus, homme de théâtre* (Oct.-Dec. 1960), 321-336.

Anderson, David. "Images of Man in Sartre and Camus." *Modern Churchman*, 8 (Oct. 1964), 33-45.

_____. "The Sisyphean Hero." In *The Tragic Protest: A Christian Study of Some Modern Literature*. London: SCM Press, 1969, pp. 82-103.

Archambault, Paul. "Augustin et Camus." *Recherches Augustiniennes*, 6 (1969), 193-221.

_____. *Camus' Hellenic Sources*. Univ. of North Carolina Studies in the Romance Langs. and Lits., No. 119. Chapel Hill: Univ. of North Carolina Press, 1972, 173pp.

Arendt, Hannah. "L'Existentialisme français vu de New York." *Deucalion*, No. 2 (1947), pp. 247-252.

_____. "La philosophie de l'existence." *Deucalion*, No. 2 (1947), pp. 214-245.

Arnaud, Pierre. "Aftermath--A Young Philosopher's View." *Yale French Studies*, No. 16, *Foray through Existentialism* (Winter 1955-1956), pp. 106-110.

Aron, Raymond. "Révolte et Révolution." In *L'Opium des intellectuels*. Coll. "Liberté de l'Esprit." Paris: Calmann-Lévy, 1955, pp. 62-69.

Astorg, Bertrand d'. "L'homme engagé: de *La Peste* ou d'un nouvel humanitarisme." *Esprit*, 15, No. 10 (Oct. 1947), 615-621.

Audisio, Gabriel. "Le génie de l'Afrique du Nord de saint Augustin à Albert Camus." *Annales du Centre universitaire méditerranéen*, 7 (1953-1954), 151-162.

Ayer, A. J. "Novelist-Philosophers, VIII: Albert Camus." Horizon, 13, No. 75 (March 1946), 155-168.

_____. "Reflexions on Existentialism." Modern Languages, 48, No. 1 (March 1967), 1-12.

Balakian, Anna. "Alienation and Aridity: The Climatic Correlative in Camus' Writings." Proceedings of the Comparative Literature Symposium [Texas Tech Univ.], 8, Albert Camus' Literary Milieu: Arid Lands (Jan. 1975), 37-52.

Barjon, Louis. "Albert Camus: La Chute." Etudes, 89, No. 291 (Oct.-Nov.-Dec. 1956), 47-59.

_____. "Le monde de l'absurde: Camus." In Mondes d'écrivains. Coll. "Destinées d'hommes." Paris: Castermann, 1960, pp. 195-210.

_____. "Le silence de Dieu dans la littérature contemporaine." Etudes, 87, No. 281 (April-May-June 1954), 178-303.

Barnes, Hazel E. "Balance and Tension in the Philosophy of Camus." The Personalist, 41, No. 4 (Oct. 1960), 433-447.

_____. Humanistic Existentialism: The Literature of Possibility. Bison Books, 145. Lincoln: Univ. of Nebraska Press, 1962, x-418pp.

Barry, Catherine. "The Concepts of Community and Christology in Camus' The Fall." Christianity and Literature, 25, No. 2 (1976), 37-42.

Barthes, Roland. "L'Etranger, roman solaire." Club, No. 12 (April 1954), pp. 6-7.

_____. "La Peste: Annales d'une épidémie ou roman de la solitude." Club, No. 21 (Feb. 1955), pp. 4-6, 8.

Bataille, Georges. "Le bonheur, le malheur et la morale d'Albert Camus." Critique, 5, No. 33 (Feb. 1949), 184-189.

_____. "La morale du malheur: La Peste." Critique, 3, Nos. 13-14 (June-July 1947), 3-15.

_____. "Le temps de la révolte (I)." Critique, 7, No. 55 (Dec. 1951), 1019-1027.

_____. "Le temps de la révolte (II)." Critique, 8, No. 56 (Jan. 1952), 29-41.

Batchelor, R. "Dostoevski and Camus: Similarities and Contrasts." Journal of European Studies, 5 (1975), 111-151.

Beauvoir, Simone de. "Chapitre V." La Force des choses. Le Livre de Poche. Paris: Gallimard, 1963. I, 325-378.

Béguin, Albert. "Albert Camus, la révolte et le bonheur." Esprit, 20, No. 4 (April 1952), 736-746.

Beigbeder, Marc. "Le monde n'est pas absurde." Esprit, 13, No. 3 (Feb. 1945), 415-419.

_____. "Le théâtre à l'âge métaphysique." L'Age Nouveau, 9, No. 85 (Jan. 1954), 30-41.

Bernard, Marc. "La contradiction d'Albert Camus." La Nouvelle Revue Française, 8, No. 87, Hommage à Albert Camus (March 1960), 594-596.

Bertman, Martin A. "Existenz Politics: Camus and Sartre." Agora, 1, No. 1 (1969), 23-32.

Bespaloff, Rachel. "Le monde du condamné à mort." Esprit, 18, No. 1, Les Carrefours de Camus (Jan. 1950), 1-26.

_____. "Réflexions sur l'esprit de la tragédie." Deucalion, No. 2 (1947), pp. 171-193.

Blanchet, André. "L'Homme Révolté d'Albert Camus." Etudes, 85, No. 272 (Jan.-Feb.-March 1952), 48-60.

_____. "Le pari d'Albert Camus." Etudes, 93, No. 305 (April-May-June 1960), 183-199, 330-344.

Blanchot, Maurice. "La confession dédaigneuse." La Nouvelle Nouvelle Revue Française, 4, No. 48 (Dec. 1956), 1050-1056.

_____. "Le détour vers la simplicité." La Nouvelle Revue Française, 8, No. 89 (May 1960), 925-937.

_____. "Le Mythe de Sisyphe." In Faux pas. Paris: Gallimard, 1943, pp. 70-76.

_____. "Le roman de L'Etranger." In Faux pas.

Paris: Gallimard, 1943, pp. 256-261.

_____. "Réflexions sur l'enfer." La Nouvelle Nouvelle Revue Française, 2, No. 16 (April 1954), 677-686.

_____. "Réflexions sur le nihilisme." La Nouvelle Nouvelle Revue Française, 2, No. 17 (May 1954), 850-859.

_____. "Tu peux tuer cet homme." La Nouvelle Nouvelle Revue Française, 2, No. 18 (June 1954), 1059-1069.

Blanzat, Jean. "Première rencontre." La Nouvelle Revue Française, 8, No. 87, Hommage à Albert Camus (March 1960), 427-431.

Blin, Georges. "Albert Camus et l'idée de révolte." Fontaine, 10, No. 53 (June 1946), 109-117.

_____. "Albert Camus ou le sens de l'absurde." Fontaine, 5, No. 30 (Feb. 1943), 553-561.

Block, Haskell M. "Albert Camus: Towards a Definition of Tragedy." University of Toronto Quarterly, 119, No. 4 (July 1950), 354-360.

_____. "Spiritual Regeneration in the Work of Camus." Proceedings of the Comparative Literature Symposium [Texas Tech Univ.], 8, Albert Camus' Literary Milieu: Arid Lands (Jan. 1975), 71-82.

Boisdeffre, Pierre de. "Albert Camus ou l'expérience tragique." Etudes, 83, No. 267 (Oct.-Nov.-Dec. 1950), 303-325.

_____. "L'évolution spirituelle d'Albert Camus." Ecclesia, No. 101 (Aug. 1957), pp. 107-112.

_____. "L'expérience tragique d'Albert Camus." Synthèses, 5, No. 55 (Dec. 1950), 61-67.

Bois-Rabot, Gérard. "Le Dieu de Camus, Sartre et Malraux." Résurrection, No. 15 (1960), pp. 313-322.

Bollnow, Otto Friedrich. "Du monde absurde à la pensée de midi: 1) La Peste (1948); 2) L'Homme révolté (1954)." Configuration Critique d'Albert Camus, II: Camus devant la critique de langue allemande. Ed. Richard Thieberger. La Revue des Lettres Modernes, Nos. 90-93 (Winter 1963), pp. 41-72.

_____. "Existentialismus." Die Sammlung, 2, No. 11 (Nov. 1947), 654-666.

_____. "Existenzialismus und Ethik." Die Sammlung, 4 (1949), 321-335.

Bonnier, Henry. Albert Camus ou la force d'être. Coll. "Singuliers et Mal Connus." Lyon: Vitte, 1959, 160pp.

Borel, Jacques. "Nature et histoire chez Albert Camus." Critique, 17, No. 169 (June 1961), 507-521.

Borel, Pierre-Marie. "Qu'est-ce que la peste et comment la combattre?" Les Cahiers de la Licorne, No. 4 (1958), pp. 25-39.

Boudot, Maurice. "L'absurde et le bonheur dans l'oeuvre d'Albert Camus." Cahiers du Sud, 39, No. 315 (1952), 291-305.

Boudot, Pierre. "La douceur de la révolte: Albert Camus." In Nietzsche et l'au-delà de la liberté: Nietzsche et les écrivains français de 1930 à 1960. Coll. "Présence et Pensée," 16. Paris: Aubier-Montaigne, 1970, pp. 63-76.

Braun, Lev. Witness of Decline: Albert Camus, Moralist of the Absurd. Rutherford, N.J.: Fairleigh Dickinson Univ. Press, 1974, 283pp.

Brée, Germaine. Camus and Sartre: Crisis and Commitment. Delta Books. New York: Dell, 1972, xi-287pp.

Brisville, Jean-Claude. Camus. Coll. "La Bibliothèque idéale." Paris: Gallimard, 1959, 297pp.

Brochier, Jean-Jacques. Albert Camus, philosophe pour classes terminales. Paris: André Balland, 1970, 178pp.

Brombert, Victor. "Camus and the Novel of the 'Absurd.'" Yale French Studies, No. 1, Critical Biography of Existentialism (Spring-Summer 1948), pp. 119-123.

_____. The Intellectual Hero: Studies in the French Novel, 1880-1955. Phoenix Books, 158. Chicago: Univ. of Chicago Press, 1964, 255pp.

_____. "'The Renegade' or the Terror of the Absolute." <u>Yale</u> <u>French</u> <u>Studies</u>, No. 25, <u>Albert</u> <u>Camus</u> (Spring 1960), pp. 81-84.

Bruckberger, Raymond-Léopold. "L'agonie spirituelle de l'Europe." <u>Revue</u> <u>Thomiste</u>, 53, No. 3 (1953), 620-636.

_____. "Une image radieuse." <u>La</u> <u>Nouvelle</u> <u>Revue</u> <u>Française</u>, 8, No. 87, <u>Hommage</u> <u>à</u> <u>Albert</u> <u>Camus</u> (March 1960), 515-521.

_____. "La Peste d'Albert Camus." <u>Le</u> <u>Cheval</u> <u>de</u> <u>Troie</u>, No. 2 (Aug.-Sept. 1947), pp. 368-376.

Brune, Jean. "Albert Camus entre les mythes de son temps et la sagesse de la Méditerranée." <u>La</u> <u>Nation</u> <u>Française</u>, Jan. 13, 1960, pp. 3, 15.

Burke, Edward L. "Camus and the Pursuit of Happiness." <u>Thought</u>, 37, No. 146 (Autumn 1962), 391-409.

Busst, A. J. L. "A Note on the Eccentric Christology of Camus." <u>French</u> <u>Studies</u>, 16, No. 1 (Jan. 1962), 45-50.

Campbell, Robert. "Existentialism in France since the Liberation." In <u>Philosophic</u> <u>Thought</u> <u>in</u> <u>France</u> <u>and</u> <u>the</u> <u>United</u> <u>States</u>: <u>Essays</u> <u>Representing</u> <u>Major</u> <u>Trends</u> <u>in</u> <u>Contemporary</u> <u>French</u> <u>and</u> <u>American</u> <u>Philosophy</u>. Ed. Marvin Farber. Buffalo: Univ. of Buffalo Publications in Philosophy, 1950, pp. 137-150.

Cappe, Jeanne. "Camus et le désert du pessimisme." <u>Revue</u> <u>Générale</u> <u>Belge</u>, 92, No. 7 (July 1956), 1589-1591.

Carazzola, Maria. "La crise de la pensée de Camus dans La Chute." <u>Comprendre</u>, Nos. 17-18 (1957), pp. 216-220.

Carrouges, Michel. "Philosophie de La Peste." <u>La</u> <u>Vie</u> <u>Intellectuelle</u>, 15, No. 7 (July 1947), 136-141.

Catesson, Jean. "A propos du <u>Malentendu</u>." <u>Cahiers</u> <u>du</u> <u>Sud</u>, 32, No. 271 (1945), 343-347.

_____. "A propos de La Peste." <u>Cahiers</u> <u>du</u> <u>Sud</u>, 35, No. 287 (1948), 144-149.

Champigny, Robert. "The Comedy of Ethics." <u>Yale</u> <u>French</u> <u>Studies</u>, No. 25, <u>Albert</u> <u>Camus</u> (Spring

1960), pp. 72-74.

──────. "Ethics and Aesthetics in The Stranger."
In Camus: A Collection of Critical Essays. Ed.
Germaine Brée. Twentieth Century Views. Spectrum
Books, 1. Englewood Cliffs, N.J.: Prentice-Hall,
1962, pp. 122-131.

──────. "Existentialism in the Modern French
Novel." Thought, 31, No. 122 (Autumn 1956), 365-384.

──────. Humanism and Human Racism: A Critical
Study of Essays by Sartre and Camus. DPL: Series
Practica, 41. The Hague: Mouton, 1972, 82pp.

──────. "Suffering and Death." Symposium, 24, No.
3, Albert Camus II (Fall 1970), 197-205.

──────. Sur un héros païen. Coll. "Les Essais,"
XCIII. Paris: Gallimard, 1959, 208pp.

Chiaromonte, Nicola. "Albert Camus and Moderation."
Partisan Review, 15, No. 10 (Oct. 1948), 1142-1145.

──────. "La résistance à l'Histoire." Preuves,
No. 110, Albert Camus (April 1960), pp. 17-20.

Clayton, Alan J. Etapes d'un itinéraire spirituel:
Albert Camus de 1937 à 1944. Archives Albert Camus, No. 2. Archives des lettres modernes, No.
122. Paris: Lettres Modernes, Minard, 1971,
86pp.

──────. "Note sur Augustin et Camus." Albert Camus 5: Journalisme et politique, l'entrée dans
l'Histoire (1938-1940). Ed. Brian T. Fitch. La
Revue des Lettres Modernes, Nos. 315-322 (1972),
pp. 267-270.

Clergerie, Bernard. "Le mal et la nostalgie de
l'être." La Revue du Caire, 44, No. 237, Albert
Camus (May 1960), 375-392.

Coffy, Robert. Dieu des athées: Marx, Sartre, Camus.
Coll. "Le Fond du problème." Lyon: Chronique Sociale de France, 1965, 175pp.

Cohen, Lionel. "Une lignée humaniste au vingtième
siècle: Roger Martin du Gard et Albert Camus."
Hebrew University Studies in Literature, 1, No. 2

(1973), 159-182.

Colin, Pierre. "Athéisme et révolte chez Camus." La Vie Intellectuelle, 24, No. 7 (July 1952), 30-51.

Copleston, Frederick C. "A. Camus: The Absurd and the Philosophy of Revolt." In Maine de Biran to Sartre: Bergson to Sartre. Vol. IX, Pt. II of A History of Philosophy. Image Books. Garden City, N.Y.: Doubleday, 1977, pp. 186-193.

_____. Contemporary Philosophy: Studies of Logical Positivism and Existentialism. London: Burns & Oates, 1956, 230pp.

_____. Existentialism and Modern Man: A Paper Read to the Aquinas Society of London on the 14th April 1948. Aquinas Papers, No. 9. London: Blackfriars Publications, 1953, 28pp.

_____. "Existentialism and Religion." Dublin Review, 220, No. 440 (Spring 1947), 50-63.

Cormeau, Nelly. "Albert Camus: La Peste." Synthèses, 2, No. 6 (June 1947), 367-372.

_____. "L'éthique d'Albert Camus." Synthèses, 14, No. 162 (Nov. 1959), 325-351.

Costa, John. "La Peste d'Albert Camus dans l'esprit catholique." La Revue de l'Université Laval, 19, No. 5 (Jan. 1965), 459-468.

Coté, Nicolas-M. "Albert Camus et l'existence de Dieu." Culture, 20, No. 3 (Sept. 1959), 268-281.

Cox, Harvey. "Albert Camus and Profanity." In The Secular City: Secularization and Urbanization in Theological Perspective. Rev. ed. New York: Macmillan, 1966, pp. 60-68.

Cox, Richard H. "Ideology, History and Political Philosophy: Camus' L'Homme Révolté." Social Research, 32, No. 1 (Spring 1965), 71-97.

Cranston, Maurice. "Albert Camus." Encounter, 28, No. 2 (Feb. 1967), 43-54.

Cruickshank, John. "Albert Camus." In The Novelist as Philosopher: Studies in French Fiction, 1935-1960. Ed. John Cruickshank. London: Oxford Univ. Press, 1962, pp. 206-229.

_____. Albert Camus and the Literature of Revolt. Galaxy Books, 43. New York: Oxford Univ. Press, 1960, xx-249pp.

_____. "Albert Camus: Sainthood Without God." In Mansions of the Spirit: Essays in Literature and Religion. Ed. George A. Panichas. New York: Hawthorn, 1967, pp. 313-324.

_____. "The Art of Allegory in La Peste." Symposium, 11, No. 1 (Spring 1957), 61-74.

_____. "Revolt and Revolution: Albert Camus." Adam, 35, Nos. 340-342 (1970), 32-40.

_____. "Revolt and Revolution: Camus and Sartre." In The Twentieth Century. Vol. VI of French Literature and its Background. Ed. John Cruickshank. Oxford Paperbacks, No. 184. London: Oxford Univ. Press, 1970, pp. 226-243.

Cryle, Peter. "La Peste et le monde concret: étude abstraite." Albert Camus 8: Camus romancier, La Peste. Ed. Brian T. Fitch. La Revue des Lettres Modernes, Nos. 479-483 (1976), pp. 9-25.

Curtis, Jerry L. "Albert Camus as Anti-Existentialist." Kentucky Romance Quarterly, 22 (1975), 111-123.

_____. "Heroic Commitment, or the Dialectics of the Leap in Kierkegaard, Sartre, and Camus." Rice University Studies, 59, No. 3 (Summer 1973), 17-26.

_____. "Thorns and Thistles: The Weltanschauungen of Voltaire and Camus." Proceedings of the Comparative Literature Symposium [Texas Tech Univ.], 8, Albert Camus' Literary Milieu: Arid Lands (Jan. 1975), 83-98.

Denat, A. "Note sur Bergson, Teilhard et Camus." Synthèses, 19, No. 216 (1964), 134-137.

Denton, David E. The Philosophy of Albert Camus: A Critical Analysis. Boston: Prime Publishers, 1967, 77pp.

Desgraupes, Pierre. "Chamfort et M. Camus." L'Arche, 2, No. 8 (Aug. 1945), 131-132.

Devaux, André-A. "Albert Camus: Le christianisme et

l'hellénisme." *Nouvelle Revue Luxembourgeoise Academia* (1970), 11-30.

_____. "Albert Camus devant le christianisme et les chrétiens." *Sciences et Esprit*, 20, No. 1 (Jan.-April 1968), 9-30.

Devismes, M., P. Cavellat, and F. Boully. *La Justice selon Albert Camus.* Melun: Imprimerie Administrative, 1959, 25pp.

Domenach, Jean-Marie. "Résurrection de la tragédie, I. Le second romantisme: Sur Camus et Sartre." In *Le Retour du tragique: Essai.* Coll. "Esprit: 'La Condition humaine.'" Paris: Editions du Seuil, 1967, pp. 215-236.

Doubrovsky, Serge. "La morale d'Albert Camus." *Preuves*, No. 116 (Oct. 1960), pp. 39-49.

_____. "Sartre and Camus: A Study in Incarceration." *Yale French Studies*, No. 25, *Albert Camus* (Spring 1960), pp. 85-92.

Duhrssen, Alfred. "Some French Hegelians." *Review of Metaphysics*, 7, No. 2 (Dec. 1953), 323-337.

Dunwoodie, Peter. "Chestov et *Le mythe de Sisyphe*." *Albert Camus 4: Sources et Influences.* Ed. Brian T. Fitch. *La Revue des Lettres Modernes*, Nos. 264-270 (1971), pp. 43-50.

Durand, R. P. *Camus ou la sainteté sans Dieu.* Marseille: C.I.T.A., 1963, 14pp.

Durfee, Harold A. "Albert Camus and the Ethic of Rebellion." *The Journal of Religion*, 38, No. 1 (Jan. 1958), 29-45.

Du Rostu, Jean. "Un Pascal sans Christ: Albert Camus." *Etudes*, 78, No. 247 (Oct.-Nov.-Dec. 1945), 48-65, 165-177.

Earl, A. J. "Albert Camus and the Christian Religion." *Modern Languages*, 54 (1973), 67-74.

Elbrecht, Joyce. "*The Stranger* and Camus' Transcendental Existentialism." *Hartford Studies in Literature*, 4 (1972), 59-80.

Engelberg, Edward. *The Unknown Distance: From Consciousness to Conscience, Goethe to Camus.* Cambridge: Harvard Univ. Press, 1972, 288pp.

Espiau de La Maëstre, André. "Albert Camus, pèlerin de l'absolu?" Les Lettres Romanes, 15, No. 1 (Feb. 1961), 3-22.

Esprit, 18, No. 1 (Jan. 1950). Les Carrefours de Camus, 1-66.

Etiemble, René. "Peste, ou péché?" Les Temps Modernes, 3, No. 26 (Nov. 1947), 911-920.

Faucon, Louis. "Commentaires, notes et variantes." In Camus, Albert. Essais. Bibliothèque de la Pléiade, 183. Ed. Roger Quilliot and Louis Faucon. Paris: Gallimard, 1965, 1410-1416, 1430-1455.

Feibleman, James K. "Camus and the Passion of Humanism." The Kenyon Review, 25, No. 2 (Spring 1963), 281-292.

Félix, Henri. "Un philosophe de l'absurde: Albert Camus." Bulletin d'Information de la Mission Laique Française, No. 33 (Feb. 1960), pp. 5-9.

Fiorioli, Elena. "L'attitude philosophique d'Albert Camus." Culture Française, No. 8 (1961), pp. 37-39.

Fitch, Brian T. L'Etranger d'Albert Camus: Un texte, ses lecteurs, leurs lectures; Etude méthodologique. Coll. "L." Paris: Larousse, 1972, 176pp.

_____. Le Sentiment d'étrangeté chez Malraux, Sartre, Camus et S. de Beauvoir: "étranger à moi-même et à ce monde". Coll. "Bibliothèque des Lettres Modernes," 5. Paris: Lettres Modernes, Minard, 1964, 232pp.

_____. "Travaux sur L'Etranger." Albert Camus 2: Langue et Langage. Ed. Brian T. Fitch. La Revue des Lettres Modernes, Nos. 212-216 (1969), pp. 149-161.

Fonda, Carlo. "Albert Camus et la religion." Culture, 29, No. 4 (Dec. 1968), 328-342.

_____. "La liberté contre les hommes." Revue de l'Université d'Ottawa, 38, No. 3 (July-Sept. 1968), 482-494.

Fontan, Antonio. "Camus entre le paganisme et le christianisme." La Table Ronde, No. 146, Albert Camus (Feb. 1960), pp. 114-119.

Fraisse, Simone. "De Lucrèce à Camus, ou les contradictions de la révolte." Esprit, 27, No. 3 (March 1959), 437-453.

Frémont, Laurent. "Albert Camus, Prométhée et le bonheur." La Revue de l'Université Laval, 19, No. 6 (Feb. 1965), 551-563.

Friedman, Maurice. "The Existentialist of Dialogue: Marcel, Camus, and Buber." In To Deny Our Nothingness: Contemporary Images of Man. London: Victor Gollancz, 1967, pp. 281-306.

Gadourek, Carina. Les Innocents et les Coupables: Essai d'exégèse de l'oeuvre d'Albert Camus. The Hague: Mouton, 1963, 246pp.

Gagnebin, Laurent. Albert Camus dans sa lumière: Essai sur l'évolution de sa pensée. Lausanne: Cahiers de la Renaissance Vaudoise, 1964, 182pp.

Gargan, Edward T. "Revolution and Morale in the Formative Thought of Albert Camus." Review of Politics, 25, No. 4 (Oct. 1963), 483-496.

Garnham, B. G. "Albert Camus: Metaphysical Revolt and Historical Action." The Modern Language Review, 62, No. 2 (April 1967), 248-255.

Gay-Crosier, Raymond. "L'absurde hypostasié aux dépens de l'espérance?" Albert Camus 5: Journalisme et politique, l'entrée dans l'Histoire (1938-1940). Ed. Brian T. Fitch. La Revue des Lettres Modernes, Nos. 315-322 (1972), pp. 189-194.

_____. "L'anarchisme mesuré de Camus." Symposium, 24, No. 3, Albert Camus II (Fall 1970), 243-253.

_____. Les Envers d'un échec: Etude sur le théâtre d'Albert Camus. Coll. "Bibliothèque des Lettres Modernes," 10. Paris: Lettres Modernes, Minard, 1967, 296pp.

_____. "Stuby, Gerhard, Recht und Solidarität im Denken von Albert Camus." Albert Camus 4: Sources et Influences. Ed. Brian T. Fitch. La Revue des Lettres Modernes, Nos. 264-270 (1971), pp. 269-276.

Gélinas, Germain-Paul. *La Liberté dans la pensée d'Albert Camus*. Coll. "SEGES," 3. Fribourg: Editions Universitaires, 1965, 177pp.

Gershman, Herbert S. "The Structure of Revolt in Malraux, Camus, and Sartre." *Symposium*, 24, No. 1 (Spring 1970), 27-35.

Ginestier, Paul. *Pour connaître la pensée de Camus*. Coll. "Pour connaître la pensée." Paris: Bordas, 1964, 206pp.

Glicksberg, Charles I. "Camus' Quest for God." *Southwest Review*, 44, No. 3 (Summer 1959), 241-250.

Gloton, R. "Albert Camus moraliste." *Lectures Culturelles*, No. 35 (Jan.-Feb. 1958), pp. 3-6.

Goedert, Georges. *Albert Camus et la question du bonheur*. Luxembourg: Edi-Centre, 1969, 120pp.

Gouhier, Henri. "Caligula d'Albert Camus." *La Vie Intellectuelle*, 13, No. 9 (Oct. 1945), 146-148.

_____. "Le Malentendu." *La Vie Intellectuelle*, 13, No. 1 (Feb. 1945), 131-132.

_____. "Sens du tragique." *La Revue Théâtrale*, No. 1 (May-June 1946), pp. 26-34.

_____. "Tragedy and Transcendence, Freedom and Poetry." *Cross Currents*, 10, No. 3 (Winter 1960), 15-28.

Green, Garret. *A Kingdom Not of this World: A Quest for a Christian Ethic of Revolution with Reference to the Thought of Dostoyevsky, Berdyaev, and Camus*. Stanford Honors Essays in Humanities, No. 8. Stanford: Stanford Univ., 1964, 37pp.

Greene, Theodore M. "Anxiety and the Search for Meaning." *Texas Quarterly*, 1, No. 3 (Summer-Autumn 1958), 172-191.

Grenier, Jean. *Albert Camus (Souvenirs)*. Paris: Gallimard, 1968, 190pp.

_____. "Un oui, un non, une ligne droite." *Le Figaro Littéraire*, Oct. 26, 1957, pp. 1, 5.

_____. "Préface." In Camus, Albert. *Théâtre, Récits, Nouvelles*. Bibliothèque de la Pléiade,

161. Ed. Roger Quilliot. Paris: Gallimard, 1962, ix-xxii.

Grenier, Roger. "Albert Camus, dix ans après: Le nietzschéen." Le Monde Hebdomadaire, Jan. 15-21, 1970.

Grobe, Edwin P. "Camus and the Parable of the Perfect Sentence." Symposium, 24, No. 3, Albert Camus II (Fall 1970), 254-261.

Guéhenno, Jean. "Mais non, la vie n'est pas absurde." Le Figaro Littéraire, Nov. 24, 1951, pp. 1, 6.

Guers-Villate, Yvonne. "Revolt and Submission in Camus and Bernanos." Renascence, 24, No. 4 (Summer 1972), 189-197.

──────. "Rieux et Daru ou le refus délibéré d'influencer autrui." Papers on Language and Literature, 3, No. 3 (Summer 1967), 229-236.

Guignet, Jean. "Deux romans existentialistes: La Nausée et L'Etranger." The French Review, 23, No. 2 (Dec. 1949), 86-91.

Guissard, Lucien. "Albert Camus ou l'humanisme tragique." Livres et Lectures, No. 73 (Dec. 1953), pp. 499-502.

Guy, Robert. "Camus, une tentative de justification de l'homme." Revue Dominicaine, 64 (July-Aug. 1958), 15-25.

Guyot, Charly. "L'humanisme d'Albert Camus." Les Cahiers Protestants, 36 (1952), 54-64.

Haggis, Donald R. Albert Camus: La Peste. Studies in French Literature, No. 9. London: Edward Arnold, 1962, 64pp.

Hall, H. Gaston. "Aspects of the Absurd." Yale French Studies, No. 25, Albert Camus (Spring 1960), pp. 26-32.

Hanna, Thomas L. "Albert Camus and the Christian Faith." The Journal of Religion, 36, No. 4 (Oct. 1956), 224-233.

──────. "Camus: Man in Revolt." In Existential Philosophers: Kierkegaard to Merleau-Ponty. New York: McGraw-Hill, 1967, pp. 331-367.

_____. *The Lyrical Existentialists*. New York: Atheneum, 1962, x-299pp.

_____. *The Thought and Art of Albert Camus*. Gateway Editions, 6053. Chicago: Henry Regnery, 1958, xxi-264pp.

Hardré, Jacques. "Camus' Thoughts on Christian Metaphysics and Neoplatonism." *Studies in Philology*, 64, No. 1 (Jan. 1967), 97-108.

Hélein-Koss, Suzanne. "Albert Camus et le Contrat social." *Studies on Voltaire and the Eighteenth Century*, 161 (1976), 165-204.

Henderickx, Paul. "Comment les personnages de *La Peste* font-ils vivre la pensée de Camus?" *Revue des Langues Vivantes: Tijdschrift voor Levende Talen*, 30, No. 2 (March-April 1964), 99-120.

_____. "Justice, amour et liberté dans la penseé d'Albert Camus." *Marche Romane*, 14 (1964), 71-80.

Henry, Patrick. "Candide as 'Etranger.'" *College Language Association Journal*, 19 (1976), 504-512.

_____. "Meursault as Antithesis of 'Homo Ludens' from J. Huizinga to Eric Berne." *Kentucky Romance Quarterly*, 21 (1974), 365-374.

_____. *Voltaire and Camus: The Limits of Reason and the Awareness of Absurdity*. Vol. CXXXVIII of *Studies on Voltaire and the Eighteenth Century*. Ed. Theodore Besterman. Banbury, Eng.: The Voltaire Foundation, 1975, 261pp.

Hervé, Pierre. "La révolte camuse." *La Nouvelle Critique*, 4, No. 35 (April 1952), 66-76.

Hochberg, Herbert. "Albert Camus and the Ethic of Absurdity." *Ethics*, 75, No. 2 (Jan. 1965), 87-102.

Hopkins, Patricia M. "Valéry and Camus: Solar Reflections." *Proceedings of the Comparative Literature Symposium* [Texas Tech Univ.], 8, *Albert Camus' Literary Milieu: Arid Lands* (Jan. 1975), 133-149.

Hourdin, Georges. *Camus le juste*. Coll. "Tout le monde en parle." Paris: Editions du Cerf, 1960, 108pp.

Jagger, George. "Camus's *La Peste*." *Yale French Stud-*

ies, No. 1, Critical Biography of Existentialism (Spring-Summer 1948), pp. 124-127.

Jeanson, Francis. "Albert Camus ou l'âme révoltée." Les Temps Modernes, 7, No. 79 (May 1952), 2070-2090.

_____. "Pour tout vous dire." Les Temps Modernes, 8, No. 82 (Aug. 1952), 354-383.

_____. "Albert Camus ou le mensonge de l'absurde." Revue Dominicaine, 53 (Feb. 1947), 104-107.

_____. "Une évolution dans la pensée de Camus." Erasme, Nos. 22-24 (Oct.-Dec. 1947), pp. 437-440.

Johnson, Patricia J. "Bergson's Le rire: Game Plan for Camus' L'étranger?" The French Review, 47 (1973), 46-56.

Jong, Pieter de. "Camus and Bonhoeffer on the Fall." Canadian Journal of Theology, 7, No. 4 (Oct. 1961), 245-257.

Joppa, Francis A. "Albert Camus ou la morale de la contradiction." Asemka, 1, No. 1 (1974), 28-40.

Judrin, Roger. "Sisyphe et le vent." La Nouvelle Revue Française, 8, No. 87, Hommage à Albert Camus (March 1960), 600-604.

Kampits, Peter. "La mort et la révolte dans la pensée d'Albert Camus." Giornale di metafisica, 23, No. 1 (Jan.-Feb. 1968), 19-28.

Kateb, George. "Camus' La Peste: A Dissenting View." Symposium, 17, No. 4 (Winter 1963), 292-303.

Kellogg, Jean Defrees. Dark Prophets of Hope: Dostoevsky, Sartre, Camus, Faulkner. Chicago: Loyola Univ. Press, 1975, 200pp.

Killinger, John. "Existentialism and Human Freedom." English Journal, 50 (1962), 303-313.

King, Adele. Camus. Writers and Critics. New York: Capricorn Books, 1971, 120pp.

Kirk, Irina. Dostoevsky and Camus. Munich: Fink, 1974, 150pp.

_____. "Dramatization of Consciousness in Camus and Dostoevsky." The Bucknell Review, 16, No. 1 (March 1968), 96-104.

Klein, Maxine. "The Philosopher-Dramatists." Drama Survey, 6, No. 3 (Spring 1968), 278-287.

Krieger, Murray. "Albert Camus: Beyond Nonentity and the Rejection of the Tragic." In The Tragic Vision. New York: Holt, Rinehart and Winston, 1960, pp. 144-153.

Kuhn, Helmut. "Existentialism: Christian and Antichristian." Theology Today, 6, No. 6 (Oct. 1949), 311-323.

Lacroix, Jean. Le Sens de l'athéisme moderne. Coll. "Cahiers de l'actualité religieuse," 8. Tournai: Casterman, 1958, 128pp.

Lamont, Rosette C. "The Anti-Bourgeois." The French Review, 34, No. 5 (April 1961), 445-453.

Lanfranchi, G. "Genèse d'une réponse à Albert Camus." Les Etudes Philosophiques, 12, No. 3 (July-Sept. 1957), 289-292.

Lansner, Kermit. "Albert Camus." The Kenyon Review, 14, No. 4 (Autumn 1952), 562-578.

Lauer, Quentin. "Albert Camus: The Revolt against Absurdity." Thought, 35, No. 136 (Spring 1960), 37-56.

Lebesque, Morvan. Camus par lui-même. Coll. "Ecrivains de toujours." Paris: Editions du Seuil, 1963, 187pp.

Lécollier, Paul. "Camus (Albert) 1913-1960." Encyclopaedia Universalis. 1968. III, 833-835.

_____. "Sur La Peste d'Albert Camus." Les Cahiers Rationalistes, No. 243 (Jan. 1967), pp. 21-48.

Lefebve, Maurice-Jean. "Deux états d'une pensée." La Nouvelle Revue Française, 8, No. 87, Hommage à Albert Camus (March 1960), 491-495.

Lepp, Ignace. "L'athéisme désespéré d'Albert Camus." In Psychanalyse de l'athéisme moderne. Paris: Grasset, 1961, pp. 245-252.

Lewis, R. W. B. "Albert Camus: The Compassionate Mind." In The Picaresque Saint: Representative Figures in Contemporary Fiction. Philadelphia: J. B. Lippincott, 1959, pp. 57-108, 299-302.

Loose, John. "The Christian as Camus's Absurd Man." The Journal of Religion, 42, No. 3 (July 1962), 203-214.

Louis, Michel. Albert Camus ou "l'homme de la terre". Fasc. II of Humanisme et Religion. Paris: Aumônerie Catholique du Lycée Jeanson de Sailly, [1965], 20pp.

Louisgrand, Jean. "L'absurde: Camus (1913-1960)." In De Lucrèce à Camus: Littérature et philosophie comme réflexion sur l'homme. Coll. "Essais et critiques," 10. Paris: Didier, 1970, pp. 319-321.

Luppé, Robert de. Albert Camus. Coll. "Classiques du XXe siècle," 1. Brussels: Editions Universitaires, 1952, 122pp.

Madariaga, Salvador de. "L'esprit et le coeur." La Nouvelle Revue Française, 8, No. 87, Hommage à Albert Camus (March 1960), 539-544.

Madaule, Jacques. "Camus et Dostoievski." La Table Ronde, No. 146, Albert Camus (Feb. 1960), pp. 127-136.

Madison, M. M. "Albert Camus: Philosopher of Limits." Modern Fiction Studies, 10, No. 3 (Autumn 1964), 223-231.

Maire, Gilbert. "Albert Camus et l'idée de révolte." La Table Ronde, No. 146, Albert Camus (Feb. 1960), pp. 75-79.

Majault, Joseph. Camus, révolte et liberté. Coll. "Humanisme et religion." Paris: Editions du Centurion, 1965, 158pp.

Malevitis, Christos. "Albert Camus, ho apostolos tou mesogeiakou metrou." Philologike Protochronia, 28 (1971), 171-185.

Marcel, Gabriel. "Albert Camus." Les Nouvelles Littéraires, Jan. 7, 1960, pp. 1, 8.

_____. "L'Homme Révolté." La Table Ronde, No.

146, Albert Camus (Feb. 1960), pp. 80-94.

Marek, Joseph C. "L'absence de Dieu et la révolte: Camus et Dostoievski." La Revue de l'Université Laval, 10, No. 6 (Feb. 1956), 490-510.

Martin, Alain-Georges. "Albert Camus et le Christianisme." La Revue Réformée, 12, No. 4 (Oct. 1961), 30-50.

Martin, Vincent. Existentialism: Kierkegaard, Sartre, and Camus. Compact Studies: Philosophy Series. Washington, D.C.: Thomist Press, 1962, 48pp.

Mason, H. A. "M. Camus and the Tragic Hero." Scrutiny, 14, No. 2 (Dec. 1946), 82-89.

Mason, Haydn T. "Voltaire and Camus." The Romanic Review, 59, No. 3 (Oct. 1968), 198-212.

Matthews, J. H. "In Which Albert Camus Makes His Leap: Le Mythe de Sisyphe." Symposium, 24, No. 3, Albert Camus II (Fall 1970), 277-288.

Matzneff, Gabriel. "'Les limites de l'humanisme athée.'" Les Nouvelles Littéraires, Jan. 1, 1970.

May, William F. "Albert Camus: Political Moralist." Christianity and Crisis, 18, No. 20 (Nov. 1958), 165-168.

Mehl, Roger. "De la révolte à la valeur." Foi et Vie, 50, No. 6 (Nov.-Dec. 1952), 516-532.

Melançon, Marcel. Albert Camus, analyse de sa pensée. Coll. "SEGES," 22. Fribourg: Editions Universitaires; Paris: Klincksieck, 1976, 280pp.

Ménard, René. "Camus et la recherche d'une légitimité." Critique, 14, Nos. 135-136 (Aug.-Sept. 1958), 675-689.

Millholland, Donald. "Albert Camus and Existentialism." Religious Humanism, 2 (Fall 1968), 162-166.

Mizicko, M. "Albert Camus and Christian Metaphysics." Duns Scotus Philosophical Association Report, 27 (1963), 116-144.

Moeller, Charles. "Albert Camus ou l'honnêteté désespérée." In Silence de Dieu. Vol. I of Littérature du XXe siècle et Christianisme. Tournai:

Casterman, 1954, pp. 25-90.

_____. "Existentialisme et pensée chrétienne."
La Revue Nouvelle, 13, No. 6 (June 1951), 570-581.

_____. "Le sens de Dieu dans la littérature moderne." Résurrection, No. 8 (1958), pp. 3-19.

Monférier, Jacques. "L'impossible dialogue: remarques sur le thème de la lucidité chez Bernanos et Camus." Revue des Sciences Humaines, 30, Fasc. 119 (July-Sept. 1965), 403-414.

Moré, Marcel. "Les racines métaphysiques de la révolte." Dieu Vivant, No. 21 (1952), pp. 35-59.

Mounier, Emmanuel. "Albert Camus ou l'appel des humiliés." Esprit, 18, No. 1, Les Carrefours de Camus (Jan. 1950), 27-66.

Natov, Nadine. "Albert Camus devant la critique soviétique." Albert Camus 8: Camus romancier, La Peste. Ed. Brian T. Fitch. La Revue des Lettres Modernes, Nos. 479-483 (1976), pp. 147-166.

Neilson, Frank P. "The Plague: Camus's Pro-Fascist Allegory." Literature & Ideology, No. 15 (1973), pp. 17-26.

Nicholson, Graeme. "Camus and Heidegger: Anarchists." University of Toronto Quarterly, 141 (1971), 14-23.

Nicolas, André. Albert Camus ou le vrai Prométhée. Coll. "Philosophes de tous les temps," 28. Paris: Editions Seghers, 1966, 190pp.

_____. Une Philosophie de l'existence: Albert Camus. Paris: Presses Universitaires de France, 1964, 193pp.

Niel, André. "Camus et le drame du Moi." Revue de la Méditerranée, 17, No. 82 (Nov.-Dec. 1957), 603-622.

_____. "L'humanisme existentialiste à travers André Malraux, Albert Camus, Jean-Paul Sartre." In Les Grands Appels de l'humanisme contemporain: Christianisme, marxisme, évolutionnisme, existentialisme . . . et après? Paris: Editions "Courrier du Livre," 1966, pp. 25-33.

O'Brien, Edward. "Camus and Christianity." The Personalist, 44, No. 2 (April 1963), 149-163.

Olafson, Frederick A. "Albert Camus: The Myth of Sisyphus." The Philosophical Review, 66, No. 1 (1957), 104-107.

Ollivier, Albert. "Albert Camus et le refus de l'éternel." L'Arche, 2, No. 6 (Oct.-Nov. 1944), 158-163.

Onimus, Jean. Camus. Coll. "Les Ecrivains devant Dieu." Paris: Desclée de Brouwer, 1965, 139pp.

_____. "D'Ubu à Caligula, ou la tragédie de l'intelligence." Etudes, 91, No. 297 (April-May-June 1958), 325-338.

Oyen, Hendrik van. "Le message du révolté." Configuration Critique d'Albert Camus, II: Camus devant la critique de langue allemande. Ed. Richard Thieberger. La Revue des Lettres Modernes, Nos. 90-93 (Winter 1963), pp. 73-89.

Paepcke, Fritz. "Le sens de l'athéisme chez Albert Camus." Configuration Critique d'Albert Camus, II: Camus devant la critique de langue allemande. Ed. Richard Thieberger. La Revue des Lettres Modernes, Nos. 90-93 (Winter 1963), pp. 91-99.

Papadopoulo, Alexandre. "Albert Camus et la bonne conscience." La Revue du Caire, 44, No. 237, Albert Camus (May 1960), 345-367.

Papamalamis, Dimitris. Albert Camus et la pensée grecque. "Collection des Mémoires," No. 11. Nancy: Publications du Centre Européen Universitaire, 1965, viii-89pp.

Parain, Brice. "Un héros de notre temps." La Nouvelle Revue Française, 8, No. 87, Hommage à Albert Camus (March 1960), 405-408.

Perrot, Jean. "Le Descartes dostoïvskien de La chute d'Albert Camus." Albert Camus 5: Journalisme et politique, l'entrée dans l'Histoire (1938-1940). Ed. Brian T. Fitch. La Revue des Lettres Modernes, Nos. 315-322 (1972), pp. 129-153.

Perruchot, Henri. "Albert Camus ou l'innocence tragique." La Pensée Française, 19, No. 3 (March 1960), 15-18.

Peuch, Jacques. "Existentialisme et biologie." La Revue du Caire, 10, No. 102 (Sept. 1947), 48-56.

Peyre, Henri. "Albert Camus: An Anti-Christian Moralist." Proceedings of the American Philosophical Society, 102, No. 5 (Oct. 1958), 477-482.

──────. "Albert Camus: Moralist and Novelist." In French Novelists of Today. Galaxy Books, 189. New York: Oxford Univ. Press, 1967, pp. 308-336.

──────. Albert Camus, moraliste. The First Kathleen Morris Scruggs Memorial Lecture. Lynchburg, Va.: Randolph-Macon College, 1962, 22pp.

──────. "Camus the Pagan." Yale French Studies, No. 25, Albert Camus (Spring 1960), pp. 20-25.

──────. "The Crisis of Modern Man as Seen by André Malraux and Albert Camus." In Historical and Critical Essays. Lincoln: Univ. of Nebraska Press, 1968, pp. 265-282.

──────. "Existentialism: A Literature of Despair?" Yale French Studies, No. 1, Critical Biography of Existentialism (Spring-Summer 1948), pp. 21-32.

──────. "Friends and Foes of Pascal in France Today." Yale French Studies, No. 12, God and the Writer (Fall-Winter 1953), pp. 8-18.

Picon, Gaëtan. "Remarques sur La Peste." Fontaine, 11, No. 61 (Sept. 1947), 453-460.

Plagnol, Maurice. "Albert Camus, esprit méditerranéen." Bulletin de l'Association Guillaume Budé, 3rd ser., No. 1 (March 1953), pp. 101-112.

Plinval, Georges de. "Les idées-pièges de l'existentialisme." Ecrits de Paris, No. 141 (Sept. 1956), pp. 57-73.

Polin, Raymond. "The Philosophy of Values in France." In Philosophic Thought in France and the United States: Essays Representing Major Trends in Contemporary French and American Philosophy. Ed. Marvin Farber. Buffalo: Univ. of Buffalo Publications in Philosophy, 1950, pp. 203-218.

Pollmann, Leo. Sartre and Camus: Literature of Existence. Trans. Helen and Gregor Sebba. New York:

Frederick Ungar, 1970, ix-253pp.

Poster, Mark. "The Confrontation with Liberalism." In *Existential Marxism in Postwar France: From Sartre to Althusser.* Princeton: Princeton Univ. Press, 1975, pp. 187-195.

Pouillon, Jean. "L'optimisme de Camus." *Les Temps Modernes*, 3, No. 26 (Nov. 1947), 921-929.

Pratt, Bruce. "Epicureanism in L'Etranger." *Essays in French Literature*, 11 (1974), 74-82.

Quilliot, Roger. "Commentaires, notes et variantes." In Camus, Albert. *Essais.* Bibliothèque de la Pléiade, 183. Ed. Roger Quilliot and Louis Faucon. Paris: Gallimard, 1965, 1220-1223, 1314-1320, 1596-1597, 1609-1662, 1886-1891, 1916-1917.

_____. *La Mer et les Prisons: Essai sur Albert Camus.* Rev. ed. Paris: Gallimard, 1970, 315pp.

_____. "Un monde ambigu." *Preuves*, No. 110, *Albert Camus* (April 1960), pp. 28-38.

Rauhut, Franz. "Du nihilisme à la 'mesure' et à l'amour des hommes." *Configuration Critique d'Albert Camus, II: Camus devant la critique de langue allemande.* Ed. Richard Thieberger. *La Revue des Lettres Modernes*, Nos. 90-93 (Winter 1963), pp. 17-40.

Reardon, B. M. G. "Albert Camus's Philosophy of Revolt." *Theology*, 63, No. 480 (June 1960), 236-242.

Reichenbach, Bruce. "Camus and Kierkegaard: A Contrast in Existential Authenticity." *University College Quarterly*, 5 (1976), 223-240.

Rideau, Emile. "L'humanisme de la révolte." In *Paganisme et Christianisme.* Tournai: Casterman, 1953, pp. 143-150.

Robbe-Grillet, Alain. "Nature, humanisme, tragédie." *La Nouvelle Nouvelle Revue Française*, 6, No. 70 (Oct. 1958), 580-604.

Romeyer, Blaise. "Le problème des autres chez Blondel, Sartre et Camus." *Giornale di metafisica*, 8, No. 2 (March-April 1953), 185-206.

Rosenthal, Bianca. "Camus and Nietzsche: Parallels and Divergences." *Proceedings of the Pacific Northwest Conference on Foreign Languages*, 25 (April 1974), 232-235.

Rossi, Louis R. "Albert Camus: The Plague of Absurdity." *The Kenyon Review*, 20, No. 3 (Summer 1958), 399-422.

Rostenne, Paul. "Sartre ou la mauvaise conscience athée." *La Revue Nouvelle*, 7, No. 4 (April 1948), 390-395.

Roth, Leon. "A Contemporary Moralist: Albert Camus." *Philosophy*, 30, No. 115 (Oct. 1955), 291-303.

Roudiez, Leon S. "Les étrangers chez Melville et Camus." *Configuration Critique d'Albert Camus, I* (3): L'Etranger à l'étranger, Camus devant la critique anglo-saxonne. Ed. J. H. Matthews. *La Revue des Lettres Modernes*, Nos. 64-66 (Autumn 1961), pp. 39-53.

Rousseaux, André. "Albert Camus et la philosophie du bonheur." *Symposium*, 2, No. 1 (May 1948), 1-18.

Roy, Claude. "Sur l'espèce humaine." *Europe*, 25, No. 22 (Oct. 1947), 99-104.

Roynet, L. "Albert Camus chez les chrétiens." *La Vie Intellectuelle*, 17, No. 4 (April 1949), 336-351.

St. Aubyn, F. C. "Albert Camus and the Death of the Other: An Existentialist Interpretation." *French Studies*, 16, No. 2 (April 1962), 124-141.

_____. "A Note on Nietzsche and Camus." *Comparative Literature*, 20 (Spring 1968), 110-116.

Saisselin, Rémy G. "The Absurd, Death, and History." *The Personalist*, 42, No. 2 (April 1961), 165-177.

Salvet, André. "La philosophie d'Albert Camus." *Méridien*, No. 8 (July-Aug. 1943), pp. 22-25.

Samson, Jean-Paul. "Humanisme et péché." *Témoins*, 5, Nos. 15-16 (Winter-Spring 1957), 17-25.

Sargent, Lyman Tower. "Prolegomena to a Study of the Political Philosophy of Albert Camus." *Minnesota Review*, 4, No. 3 (Spring 1964), 365-369.

Sarocchi, Jean. *Camus.* Coll. "'SUP': Philosophes."
Paris: Presses Universitaires de France, 1968, 126pp.

Sartre, Jean-Paul. "Albert Camus." In *Situations IV.* Paris: Gallimard, 1964, pp. 126-129.

──────. "Explication de *L'Etranger.*" In *Situations I.* Paris: Gallimard, 1947, pp. 92-112.

──────. "Réponse à Albert Camus." *Les Temps Modernes*, 8, No. 82 (Aug. 1952), 334-353. Rpt. in *Situations IV.* Paris: Gallimard, 1964, pp. 90-125.

Schneider, Peter. "Mesure et justice." *Configuration Critique d'Albert Camus, II: Camus devant la critique de langue allemande.* Ed. Richard Thieberger. *La Revue des Lettres Modernes*, Nos. 90-93 (Winter 1963), pp. 101-124.

Scott, Nathan A., Jr. *Albert Camus.* Studies in Modern European Literature and Thought. New York: Hillary House, 1963, 112pp.

──────. "The Modest Optimism of Albert Camus." *Christian Scholar*, 42, No. 4 (Dec. 1959), 251-274.

Sefler, George F. "The Existential vs. The Absurd: The Aesthetics of Nietzsche and Camus." *The Journal of Aesthetics and Art Criticism*, 32 (1974), 415-421.

Sénart, Philippe. "Camus et le juste milieu." *La Table Ronde*, Nos. 174-175 (July-Aug. 1962), pp. 112-115.

Sérant, Paul. "Réalisme et civilisation." *La Revue des Deux Mondes*, No. 22 (Nov. 1957), pp. 336-344.

Serge, Victor. "L'existentialisme." *Death*, 1, No. 1 (Summer 1946), 25-30.

Simon, Emile. *Une Métaphysique tragique.* Coll. "Espoir." Paris: Gallimard, 1951, 214pp.

Simon, Pierre-Henri. "Albert Camus entre Dieu et l'histoire." *Terre Humaine*, 2, No. 14 (Feb. 1952), 8-21.

──────. "Albert Camus et l'homme." In *Témoins de l'homme: La condition humaine dans la littérature*

du XXe siècle. Coll. "Petite Bibliothèque Payot,"
96. Paris: Payot, 1967, pp. 205-225.

_____. "Albert Camus ou l'invention de la justice." In L'Homme en procès: Malraux, Sartre, Camus, Saint-Exupéry. Coll. "Petite Bibliothèque Payot," 72. Paris: Payot, 1965, pp. 93-124.

_____. "Albert Camus et la justice." In Théâtre et Destin: La signification de la renaissance dramatique en France au XXe siècle. Paris: Armand Colin, 1959, pp. 191-211.

_____. "Camus ou le retour à l'homme." Revue Générale Belge, No. 47 (Sept. 1949), pp. 767-777.

_____. "Points de vue existentialistes sur l'histoire." In L'Esprit et l'Histoire: Essai sur la conscience historique dans la littérature du XXe siècle. Coll. "Petite Bibliothèque Payot," 144. Paris: Payot, 1969, pp. 141-180.

_____. Présence de Camus. Coll. "La Lettre et l'Esprit." Brussels: La Renaissance du Livre, 1962, 157pp.

_____. "Sartre et Camus devant l'histoire." Terre Humaine, 2, No. 23 (Nov. 1952), 9-20.

Singleton, Michael. "Teilhard on Camus." International Philosophical Quarterly, 9, No. 2 (June 1969), 236-247.

Soulié, Michel. "Albert Camus et la recherche du bonheur." Letras, No. 13 (1964), pp. 71-95.

Spens, Willy de. "Camus et le pessimisme." La Table Ronde, No. 165 (Oct. 1961), pp. 128-133.

Spiegelberg, Herbert. "French Existentialism: Its Social Philosophies." The Kenyon Review, 16, No. 3 (Summer 1954), 446-462.

Starobinski, Jean. "Dans le premier silence." La Nouvelle Revue Française, 8, No. 87, Hommage à Albert Camus (March 1960), 496-500.

Stern, Alfred. "Albert Camus (1913-1960)." Revue Philosophique de la France et de l'Etranger, 150, No. 3 (July-Sept. 1960), 423-424.

_____. "Considerations of Albert Camus' Doctrine." The Personalist, 41, No. 4 (Oct. 1960), 448-457.

Strem, George G. "The Theme of Rebellion in the Works of Camus and Dostoievsky." Revue de Littérature Comparée, 40, No. 2 (April-June 1966), 246-257.

Sturm, Ernest. Conscience et impuissance chez Dostoievski et Camus: Parallèle entre le Sous-sol et la Chute. Paris: Nizet, 1967, 125pp.

Susskind, Alexander J. "Hölderlin et Camus." Revue de Littérature Comparée, 43, No. 4 (Oct.-Dec. 1969), 489-504.

Tate, Robert S. "The Concept of Absurd Equilibrium in the Early Essays of Albert Camus." The South Atlantic Quarterly, 70, No. 3 (Summer 1971), 377-385.

Thielicke, Helmut. "The Human Form of the World's Breakdown." In Nihilism: Its Origin and Nature, with a Christian Answer. Trans. John W. Doberstein. New York: Schocken Books, 1969, pp. 96-104.

Thody, Philip. Albert Camus, 1913-1960. London: Hamish Hamilton, 1961, 242pp.

_____. Albert Camus: A Study of His Work. Evergreen Books, 143. New York: Grove Press, 1959, 155pp.

_____. "Camus et la politique." Albert Camus 2: Langue et Langage. Ed. Brian T. Fitch. La Revue des Lettres Modernes, Nos. 212-216 (1969), pp. 137-147.

Thoorens, Léon. A la rencontre d'Albert Camus. Coll. "A la rencontre de . . ." Brussels: La Sixaine, 1946, 43pp.

Thorson, Thomas Landon. "Albert Camus and the Rights of Man." Ethics, 74, No. 4 (July 1964), 281-291.

Tillich, Paul. "Existential Philosophy." Journal of the History of Ideas, 5, No. 1 (Jan. 1944), 44-70.

Treil, Claude. L'Indifférence dans l'oeuvre d'Albert Camus. Sherbrooke, Quebec: Editions Cosmos; Paris: Nizet, 1971, 171pp.

―――――. "Religion de l'indifférence chez Camus." La Revue de l'Université Laval, 20, No. 9 (May 1966), 808-815.

Troisfontaines, Roger. Existentialisme et pensée chrétienne. Louvain: J. Vrin, 1946, 92pp.

―――――. "What is Existentialism?" Thought, 32, No. 127 (Winter 1957-1958), 516-532.

Troyat, Henri. "Albert Camus: Caligula." La Nef, 2, No. 12 (Nov. 1945), 149-153.

―――――. "Réponse à Albert Camus." La Nef, 3, No. 14 (Jan. 1946), 145-148.

Ubersfeld, Annie. "Albert Camus ou la métaphysique de la contre-révolution." La Nouvelle Critique, 10, No. 92 (Jan. 1958), 110-130.

Van-Huy, Pierre Nguyen. "Camus et le problème de la dualité (I)." The University of South Florida Language Quarterly, 8, Nos. 1-2 (Fall-Winter 1969), 9-15.

―――――. "Camus et le problème de la dualité (II)." The University of South Florida Language Quarterly, 8, Nos. 3-4 (Spring-Summer 1970), 37-47.

―――――. "Camus et la responsabilité." The University of South Florida Language Quarterly, 13, Nos. 3-4 (Spring-Summer 1975), 19-26.

―――――. "Camus et la transcendance." The University of South Florida Language Quarterly, 7, Nos. 3-4 (Spring-Summer 1969), 5-10.

―――――, and Phan Thi Ngoc-Mai. La Chute de Camus ou le dernier testament: Etude du message camusien de responsabilité et d'authenticité selon La Chute. With the collaboration of Jean-René Peltier. Coll. "Langages." Neuchâtel: La Baconnière, 1974, 241pp.

―――――. "La Chute: 'Somme philosophique' camusienne." The University of South Florida Language Quarterly, 11, Nos. 1-2 (Fall-Winter 1972), 2-10.

―――――. "Clamence ou le grand messager camusien (I)." The University of South Florida Language Quarterly, 14, Nos. 1-2 (Fall-Winter 1975), 23-25.

──────. "Clamence ou le grand messager camusien (II)." The University of South Florida Language Quarterly, 14, Nos. 3-4 (Spring-Summer 1976), 5-9, 12.

──────. "Clamence ou le grand messager camusien (III)." The University of South Florida Language Quarterly, 15, Nos. 1-2 (Fall-Winter 1976), 47-51.

──────. "L'Etranger ou le conflit des valeurs." The University of South Florida Language Quarterly, 11, Nos. 3-4 (Spring-Summer 1973), 23-26.

──────. La Métaphysique du bonheur chez Albert Camus. 2nd ed. Coll. "Langages." Neuchâtel: La Baconnière, 1968, xvii-248pp.

Velikovski, Samari. "La Peste d'Albert Camus." Recherches Internationales à la Lumière du Marxisme, 9, No. 50 (Nov.-Dec. 1965), 142-174.

Veubeke, Jean de. "L'absurde aujourd'hui." Solstice, No. 1 (Autumn 1945), pp. 20-27.

Viallaneix, Paul. "L''incroyance passionnée' d'Albert Camus." Albert Camus 1: Autour de L'Etranger. Ed. Brian T. Fitch. La Revue des Lettres Modernes, Nos. 170-174 (1968), pp. 179-197.

Viatte, Auguste. "Albert Camus devant l'athéisme." La Revue de l'Université Laval, 6, No. 8 (April 1952), 642-647.

Vigée, Claude. "La nostalgie du sacré chez Albert Camus." La Nouvelle Revue Française, 8, No. 87, Hommage à Albert Camus (March 1960), 527-536.

Viggiani, Carl A. "Camus and the Fall from Innocence." Yale French Studies, No. 25, Albert Camus (Spring 1960), pp. 65-71.

Weinberg, Kurt. "The Theme of Exile." Yale French Studies, No. 25, Albert Camus (Spring 1960), pp. 33-40.

Welton, Donn A. "Albert Camus and the Tragic Vision of Existence." Kinesis, 1, No. 2 (Spring 1969), 65-74.

Werner, Eric. De la violence au totalitarisme: Essai sur la pensée de Camus et de Sartre. Coll. "Liberté de l'Esprit." Paris: Calmann-Lévy, 1972,

261pp.

Wild, Alfred. "La philosophie de l'absurde." Suisse Contemporaine, No. 12 (Dec. 1945), pp. 1136-1149.

Willhoite, Fred H., Jr. Beyond Nihilism: Albert Camus's Contribution to Political Thought. Baton Rouge: Louisiana State Univ. Press, 1968, xi-225pp.

Williams, Thomas A., Jr. "Albert Camus and the Two Houses of Descartes." Romance Notes, 5, No. 2 (Spring 1964), 115-117.

Woelfel, James W. Camus: A Theological Perspective. Nashville: Abington Press, 1975, 142pp.

Wollheim, Richard. "The Political Philosophy of Existentialism." The Cambridge Journal, 7, No. 1 (Oct. 1953), 3-19.

Wurmser, André. "Préface à La Peste." La Nouvelle Critique, 16, No. 160 (Nov. 1964), 92-110.

Zéraffa, Michel. "Aspects structuraux de l'absurde dans la littérature contemporaine." Journal de Psychologie Normale et Pathologique, 61, No. 4 (Oct.-Dec. 1964), 437-456.

Ziolkowski, Theodore. "Camus in Germany, or the Return of the Prodigal Son." Yale French Studies, No. 25, Albert Camus (Spring 1960), pp. 132-137.

IV. Other Works Consulted

Aron, Raymond. "The Philosophy of History." In Philosophic Thought in France and the United States: Essays Representing Major Trends in Contemporary French and American Philosophy. Ed. Marvin Farber. Buffalo: Univ. of Buffalo Publications in Philosophy, 1950, pp. 301-320.

Barrett, William. Irrational Man: A Study in Existential Philosophy. Anchor Books, 321. Garden City, N.Y.: Doubleday, 1958, 314pp.

Beauvoir, Simone de. Pour une morale de l'ambiguïté suivi de Pyrrhus et Cinéas. Coll. "Idées," 21. Paris: Gallimard, 1969, 370pp.

Benda, Julien. Kant. Coll. "Les Classiques de la Liberté," 7. Geneva: Editions des Trois Collines, 1948, 163pp.

Berdyaev, Nicolas. The Destiny of Man. Trans. Natalie Duddington. Harper Torchbooks, 61. New York: Harper & Row, 1960, viii-310pp.

_____. Dream and Reality: An Essay in Autobiography. Trans. Katharine Lampert. New York: Macmillan, 1951, xv-332pp.

Berlin, Isaiah. The Age of Enlightenment: The 18th Century Philosophers. The Mentor Philosophers Series. Mentor Books. New York: New American Library, 1956, 282pp.

_____. Vico and Herder: Two Studies in the History of Ideas. Vintage Books, 250. New York: Random House, 1977, xxvii-228pp.

Cassirer, Ernst. The Philosophy of the Enlightenment. Trans. Fritz C. A. Koelln and James P. Pettegrove. Princeton: Princeton Univ. Press, 1951, xiii-366pp.

_____. Rousseau, Kant, Goethe: Two Essays. Trans. James Gutmann, Paul Oskar Kristeller, and John Herman Randall, Jr. Princeton Paperbacks, 195. Princeton: Princeton Univ. Press, 1970, xvii-98pp.

Clarence, E. "Kant, Heidegger, Sartre et la querelle de l'humanisme." La Parisienne, No. 12 (Dec. 1953), pp. 1604-1612.

Copleston, Frederick C. Maine de Biran to Sartre: The Revolution to Henri Bergson. Vol. IX, Pt. I of A History of Philosophy. Image Books. Garden City, N.Y.: Doubleday, 1977, 280pp.

_____. Maine de Biran to Sartre: Bergson to Sartre. Vol. IX, Pt. II of A History of Philosophy. Image Books. Garden City, N.Y.: Doubleday, 1977, 277pp.

Crocker, Lester G. An Age of Crisis: Man and World in Eighteenth Century French Thought. The Goucher College Series. Baltimore: The Johns Hopkins Press, 1959, xx-496pp.

_____. Nature and Culture: Ethical Thought in the French Enlightenment. Baltimore: The Johns

Hopkins Press, 1963, xx-540pp.

_____. "The Discussion of Suicide in the Eighteenth Century." Journal of the History of Ideas, 13, No. 1 (Jan. 1952), 47-72.

Curtis, Jerry L. "Candide et le principe d'action: Développement d'un méliorisme chez Voltaire." Romanische Forschungen, 86 (1974), 57-71.

De Waelhens, Alphonse. Phénoménologie et Vérité. 3rd ed. Louvain: Editions Nauwelaerts; Paris: Béatrice-Nauwelaerts, 1969, 160pp.

Dieckmann, Herbert. "On Interpretations of the Eighteenth Century." Modern Language Quarterly, 15, No. 4 (Dec. 1954), 295-311.

Evdokimov, Paul. The Struggle With God. Trans. Sister Gertrude, S.P. Exploration Books. Glen Rock, N.J.: Paulist Press, 1966, vi-218pp.

Fellows, Otis E., and Norman L. Torrey. "General Introduction." In The Age of Enlightenment: An Anthology of Eighteenth Century French Literature. Ed. Otis E. Fellows and Norman L. Torrey. New York: Appleton-Century-Crofts, 1942, pp. 1-18.

Flam, Léopold. La Philosophie au tournant de notre temps. Brussels: Presses Universitaires de Bruxelles, 1970, 214pp.

Gay, Peter. The Enlightenment, An Interpretation: The Rise of Modern Paganism. The Norton Library, 870. New York: W. W. Norton, 1977, xviii-555-xvpp.

_____. "Introduction." In Cassirer, Ernst. Rousseau, Kant, Goethe: Two Essays. Trans. James Gutmann, Paul Oskar Kristeller, and John Herman Randall, Jr. Princeton Paperbacks, 195. Princeton: Princeton Univ. Press, 1970, pp. ix-xv.

Giannaras, Christos. "An Orthodox Comment on 'The Death of God.'" Sobornost, 5th ser., No. 4 (Winter 1966), pp. 249-257.

Gleason, Abbott. European and Muscovite: Ivan Kireevsky and the Origins of Slavophilism. Russian Research Center Studies, 68. Cambridge: Harvard Univ. Press, 1972, x-376pp.

Goldmann, Lucien. Le Dieu caché: Etude sur la vision

tragique dans les Pensées de Pascal et dans le théâtre de Racine. Coll. "Bibliothèque des Idées." Paris: Gallimard, 1959, 454pp.

Grimsley, Ronald. "Irony in Voltaire and Kierkegaard." In From Montesquieu to Laclos: Studies on the French Enlightenment. Histoire des Idées et Critique Littéraire, 141. Geneva: Droz, 1974, pp. 125-131.

_____. "Preface." In From Montesquieu to Laclos: Studies on the French Enlightenment. Histoire des Idées et Critique Littéraire, 141. Geneva: Droz, 1974, p. 1.

Haac, Oscar. "Voltaire and Leibnitz: Two Aspects of Rationalism." Studies on Voltaire and the Eighteenth Century, 25 (1963), 795-809.

Hendel, Charles W., ed. The Philosophy of Kant and Our Modern World: Four Lectures Delivered at Yale University Commemorating the 150th Anniversary of the Death of Immanuel Kant. New York: The Liberal Arts Press, 1957, 132pp.

Janik, Allan, and Stephen Toulmin. Wittgenstein's Vienna. Touchstone Books. New York: Simon and Schuster, 1973, 314pp.

Kant, Immanuel. Critique of Pure Reason. Trans. J. M. D. Meiklejohn. Everyman's Library, No. 1909. London: J. M. Dent; New York: E. P. Dutton, 1934, xxxiv-483pp.

_____. Kant: Selections. Ed. Theodore Meyer Greene. Lyceum Editions: Philosophy Series, 307. New York: Charles Scribner's Sons, 1957, lxxi-526pp.

_____. Prolegomena to Any Future Metaphysics. Ed. Lewis White Beck. The Library of Liberal Arts, 27. Indianapolis: Bobbs-Merrill, 1950, xxiv-136pp.

Kaufmann, Walter. Hegel: A Reinterpretation. Anchor Books, 528a. Garden City, N.Y.: Doubleday, 1966, xxvii-405pp.

Lefebvre, Henri. Le Marxisme. Coll. "Que sais-je?", 300. Paris: Presses Universitaires de France, 1948, 127pp.

Lindsay, A. D. "Introduction." In Kant, Immanuel. *Critique of Pure Reason.* Trans. J. M. D. Meiklejohn. Everyman's Library, No. 1909. London: J. M. Dent; New York: E. P. Dutton, 1934, pp. vii-xx.

Lossky, Vladimir. *The Mystical Theology of the Eastern Church.* London: James Clarke, 1957, 252pp.

Löwith, Karl. *From Hegel to Nietzsche: The Revolution in Nineteenth-Century Thought.* Trans. David E. Green. Anchor Books, 553. Garden City, N.Y.: Doubleday, 1967, xii-468pp.

——————. *Meaning in History.* Phoenix Books, 16. Chicago: Univ. of Chicago Press, 1949, vii-259pp.

Lovejoy, Arthur O. *The Great Chain of Being, A Study of the History of an Idea: The William James Lectures Delivered at Harvard University, 1933.* Cambridge: Harvard Univ. Press, 1964, ix-382pp.

Macquarrie, John. *Existentialism.* Pelican Books. Baltimore: Penguin Books, 1973, xi-252pp.

Makrakis, Apostolos. *The City of Zion, or The Church Built Upon the Rock, i.e., The Human Society in Christ.* Trans. Denver Cummings. Chicago: The Orthodox Christian Educational Society, 1958, ii-106pp.

——————. *Introduction to Philosophy; Psychology; Logic; Theology; Philosophy.* Vol. I of *A New Philosophy and the Philosophical Sciences.* Trans. Denver Cummings. Ed. K. Andronis and P. Vassilakos. New York: G. P. Putnam's Sons, 1940, xlviii-843pp.

——————. *Ethics.* Vol. II of *A New Philosophy and the Philosophical Sciences.* Trans. Albert George Alexander. Ed. K. Andronis and P. Vassilakos. New York: G. P. Putnam's Sons, 1940, xxviii-716pp.

Miller, Eugene F. "Hayek's Critique of Reason." *Modern Age,* 20, No. 4 (Fall 1976), 383-394.

Molnar, Thomas. "In the Shadow of Nietzsche." *Modern Age,* 22, No. 3 (Summer 1978), 257-264.

——————. "Philosophical Disorder." *The Intercollegiate Review,* 11, No. 1 (Fall 1975), 25-31.

Morot-Sir, Edouard. La Pensée française d'aujourd'hui. Coll. "'SUP': Le Philosophe," 100. Paris: Presses Universitaires de France, 1971, 131pp.

Naves, Raymond. "Introduction." In Voltaire. Lettres philosophiques ou Lettres anglaises avec le texte complet des remarques sur les Pensées de Pascal. Ed. Raymond Naves. Coll. "Classiques Garnier." Paris: Garnier Frères, 1964, pp. i-xvi.

Pascal, Blaise. Pensées. Ed. Ch.-M. des Granges. Coll. "Classiques Garnier." Paris: Garnier Frères, 1964, x-342pp.

Perkins, Jean A. The Concept of the Self in the French Enlightenment. Histoire des Idées et Critique Littéraire, 94. Geneva: Droz, 1969, 162pp.

Peyre, Henri. "The Influence of Eighteenth-Century Ideas on the French Revolution." Journal of the History of Ideas, 10, No. 1 (Jan. 1949), 63-87. Rpt. in Historical and Critical Essays. Lincoln: Univ. of Nebraska Press, 1968, pp. 62-87.

―――――. L'Influence des littératures antiques sur la littérature française moderne: Etat des travaux. Yale Romanic Studies, XIX. New Haven: Yale Univ. Press, 1941, 108pp.

Popper, Karl R. The Poverty of Historicism. Harper Torchbooks, 1126. New York: Harper & Row, 1964, x-166pp.

―――――. The Spell of Plato. Vol. I of The Open Society and Its Enemies. 5th ed., rev. Princeton: Princeton Univ. Press, 1966, xi-361pp.

―――――. The High Tide of Prophecy: Hegel, Marx, and the Aftermath. Vol. II of The Open Society and Its Enemies. 5th ed., rev. Princeton: Princeton Univ. Press, 1966, v-420pp.

Prosch, Harry. The Genesis of Twentieth Century Philosophy: The Evolution of Thought from Copernicus to the Present. Apollo Editions, 296. New York: Thomas Y. Crowell, 1964, xi-418pp.

Randall, John Herman, Jr. From the German Enlightenment to the Age of Darwin. Vol. II of The Career of Philosophy. New York: Columbia Univ. Press, 1965, xii-675pp.

Runes, Dagobert D., ed. Dictionary of Philosophy. Totowa, N.J.: Littlefield, Adams, 1962, 343pp.

Sartre, Jean-Paul. "A propos de l'existentialisme: Mise au point." In Contat, Michel, and Michel Rybalka. Les Ecrits de Sartre: Chronologie, bibliographie commentée. Paris: Gallimard, 1970, pp. 653-658.

_____. L'Etre et le Néant: Essai d'ontologie phénoménologique. Coll. "Bibliothèque des Idées." Paris: Gallimard, 1943, 722pp.

_____. L'Existentialisme est un humanisme. Coll. "Pensées." Paris: Les Editions Nagel, 1968, 141pp.

_____. "Une idée fondamentale de la phénoménologie de Husserl: l'intentionnalité." In Situations I. Paris: Gallimard, 1947, pp. 29-32.

_____. La Nausée. Coll. "Folio," 46. Paris: Gallimard, 1938, 248pp.

_____. Questions de méthode. In Critique de la raison dialectique (précédé de Questions de méthode), Tome I: Théorie des ensembles pratiques. Coll. "Bibliothèque des Idées." Paris: Gallimard, 1960, pp. 13-111.

Schlobach, Jochen. "Pessimisme des philosophes? La Théorie cyclique de l'histoire au 18e siècle." Studies on Voltaire and the Eighteenth Century, 155 (1976), 1971-1987.

Shklar, Judith N. After Utopia: The Decline of Political Faith. Princeton: Princeton Univ. Press, 1957, x-309pp.

Simon, Pierre-Henri. L'Esprit et l'Histoire: Essai sur la conscience historique dans la littérature du XXe siècle. Coll. "Petite Bibliothèque Payot," 144. Paris: Payot, 1969, 204pp.

Spengler, Oswald. Form and Actuality. Vol. I of The Decline of the West. Trans. Charles Francis Atkinson. Borzoi Books. New York: Alfred A. Knopf, 1926, xv-428-xxxipp.

_____. Perspectives of World-History. Vol. II of The Decline of the West. Trans. Charles Francis Atkinson. Borzoi Books. New York: Alfred A.

Knopf, 1928, viii-507-xxxiipp.

_____. The Hour of Decision, Part One: Germany and World-Historical Evolution. Trans. Charles Francis Atkinson. Borzoi Books. New York: Alfred A. Knopf, 1934, xvi-230-xiiipp.

Temmer, Mark J. "Rousseau and Thoreau." In Art and Influence of Jean-Jacques Rousseau: The Pastoral, Goethe, Gottfried Keller, and Other Essays. Univ. of North Carolina Studies in Comp. Lit., No. 56. Chapel Hill: Univ. of North Carolina Press, 1973, pp. 93-103, 123-124.

Voltaire. Dictionnaire philosophique. Ed. Etiemble, Raymond Naves, and Julien Benda. Coll. "Classiques Garnier." Paris: Garnier Frères, 1967, xl-632pp.

_____. Lettres philosophiques ou Lettres anglaises avec le texte complet des remarques sur les Pensées de Pascal. Ed. Raymond Naves. Coll. "Classiques Garnier." Paris: Garnier Frères, 1964, xx-304pp.

_____. Romans et Contes. Ed. Henri Bénac. Coll. "Classiques Garnier." Paris: Garnier Frères, 1960, xii-675pp.

Vyverberg, Henry. Historical Pessimism in the French Enlightenment. Harvard Historical Monographs, XXXVI. Cambridge: Harvard Univ. Press, 1958, viii-253pp.

Wade, Ira O. The Intellectual Origins of the French Enlightenment. Princeton: Princeton Univ. Press, 1971, xxi-678pp.

Waterman, Mina. Voltaire, Pascal and Human Destiny. Octagon Books. New York: Farrar, Straus & Giroux, 1971, xvi-130pp.

White, Morton. The Age of Analysis: 20th Century Philosophers. The Mentor Philosophers Series. Mentor Books. New York: New American Library, 1955, 253pp.

Addenda

Berlin, Isaiah. *The Hedgehog and the Fox: An Essay on Tolstoy's View of History*. Touchstone Books. New York: Simon and Schuster, 1953, 86pp.

Cassirer, Ernst. *An Essay On Man: An Introduction to a Philosophy of Human Culture*. New Haven: Yale Univ. Press, 1944, ix-237pp.

Lévy, Bernard-Henri. *Barbarism with a Human Face*. Trans. George Holoch. New York: Harper & Row, 1979, xii-210pp.

Weaver, Richard M. *Ideas Have Consequences*. Phoenix Books, 44. Chicago: Univ. of Chicago Press, 1948, vii-190pp.

VERSITY LIBRARY
Ple   k as soon as you have